Brokering Billions

Praise for Brokering Billions™

I have known Bonneau since we were fraternity brothers at the University of Georgia. From the moment we met, I could tell he had a contagious personality and was always thinking about the next big venture. As we have grown and developed a close friendship, I have watched Bonneau grow his business at a remarkable rate.

I am used to being under pressure to generate results, so I can understand better than anyone what it means to perform at a high level. I love Bonneau's work ethic, dedication, insight, and focus on constantly getting better. I try to ensure my players have the same perspective on the field as Bonneau does off the field. *Brokering Billions* is the culmination of what Bonneau has been preaching and doing for most of his professional career. Bonneau is a force of nature and one of the most successful businessmen I know.

—Kirby Smart,
NCAA National Championship Winning Football Coach

Throughout my career in both professional football and in business, I have come across a lot of really good salespeople. I can't tell you, from years of firsthand experience, Bonneau is literally one of the best. He is intuitive, relatable, and has the ability to connect with most everyone with whom he meets.

The lessons and resources in his new book are tried and true, tested over the course of his entire career. I know they will help young agents hone the most important skill sets needed to succeed, veteran agents optimize their focus and abilities, and provide us all with a great deal of insight so we may all become experts in our respected industries.

—Fran Tarkenton,
Pro Football Hall of Fame Quarterback,
Author, Entrepreneur, and Investor

There's no better way to become successful than to learn from the most successful people in your industry. In *Brokering Billions*, Bonneau Ansley delivers exactly what you need to produce more while working less—and even enjoying your life. From setting your vision to developing a billion-dollar mindset and building the habits necessary to turn your vision into your reality, *Brokering Billions* brings you behind the scenes to how Bonneau and other top agents achieve consistent success no matter what the market looks like.

—Thad Wong,
Co-Founder and Co-CEO, @properties,
Christie's International Real Estate

Brokering Billions

Bonneau Ansley

PANTA PRESS
A BRANDED IMPRINT OF MORGAN JAMES

NEW YORK

LONDON • NASHVILLE • MELBOURNE • VANCOUVER

Brokering Billions

Secrets of the Nation's Top Real Estate Agents

Published in New York, New York, by Panta Press, a branded imprint of Morgan James Publishing. Morgan James is a trademark of Morgan James, LLC. www.MorganJamesPublishing.com

Proudly distributed by Ingram Publisher Services.

Morgan James BOGO™

A **FREE** ebook edition is available for you or a friend with the purchase of this print book.

CLEARLY SIGN YOUR NAME ABOVE

Instructions to claim your free ebook edition:
1. Visit MorganJamesBOGO.com
2. Sign your name CLEARLY in the space above
3. Complete the form and submit a photo of this entire page
4. You or your friend can download the ebook to your preferred device

ISBN 9781636981055 paperback
ISBN 9781636981062 ebook
Library of Congress Control Number:
2022949929

Cover Design by:
John Stapleton

Interior Design by:
Christopher Kirk
www.GFSstudio.com

Morgan James is a proud partner of Habitat for Humanity Peninsula and Greater Williamsburg. Partners in building since 2006.

Get involved today! Visit: www.morgan-james-publishing.com/giving-back

Dedication

*To Jen who is the greatest partner I could have asked for
in business and in life. Thank you for your unwavering support
from the very beginning all the way through my craziest ideas.*

*To Beau and Blakely, thank you for giving me the love and
driving motivation to create a life where I could work and also
be at your games. I hope that you, too, will find inspiration
and guidance in this book as you go off into the world.
I could not have brokered billions without you all!*

Table of Contents

Acknowledgments

I owe a big debt of gratitude to so many people for helping me make this book possible. As you'll read in the book, I am successful in what I do, in large part, because I surround myself with people who are the best-of-the-best at what they do.

A huge thank you to my partner in all things we have set up to support agents through *Brokering Billions*, Chris Tuff. When you and I first spoke about my passion for helping agents, you instantly helped me recognize what's possible. You then put together the team of experts to help me make the programs I've been doing with Team Bonneau and at Ansley | Christie's International Real Estate accessible to agents all over the world. That we have been able to impact so many agents even before this book is released is a testimony to just how many people we will be able to help. The best is truly yet to come!

Thank you to Thad Wong, Mark Spain, Glennda Baker, Johnny Ussery, Keene Reese, Holly Parker, Jonathan Spears, Julie Faupel, Rob Thomson, Leigh Marcus, Josh Anderson, and Elizabeth DeWoody for your willingness to share some of your top strategies for *Brokering Billions* with agents around the world.

Thank you to Jesse Itzler for your inspiration and support throughout the years as well as taking the time to write the foreword to this book to help me connect this message with even more agents.

Thank you Tyler Hartsook for all the hard work you have done behind the scenes to keep the book, podcast, and other projects we're building moving forward.

Thank you to John Stapleton for the incredible design work on the cover of this book.

Thank you to Nick Pavlidis, my book and publishing consultant, for creating and executing a plan to make *Brokering Billions* the go-to curriculum for agents who want to build a better business without burning out. Also, thank you to the talented copyeditor, Catherine Turner, whose attention to detail helped make the content clean and clear.

Thank you to Justin Spizman for helping me start this process. Your insights and passion have been a big asset in this project.

Thank you to my sister, Fayne Ansley, for spending countless hours helping me collect my thoughts and stories. Your brilliance and love for your brother were recognized throughout this process.

To my loving parents, Sharon and Bonneau Ansley. Thank you for your love and support not only sending me through school, even though I know that was challenging, but also giving me the necessary tools I needed to pursue my dreams of building my business and supporting my team and community.

A special thanks to my partner at Team Bonneau, Hil Harper, and our incredible support staff of Leslie Martin and Emily Niles. We would not be successful without your incredible contributions day in and day out.

Thank you Team Bonneau and my team at Ansley | Christie's International Real Estate. The support you provide and work we do together doesn't only help me sell more real estate, it helps me give back to our community and build projects like *Brokering Billions* to help even more people around the world. That impact will only grow as more agents apply the concepts in this book and related curriculum.

And, last but not least, thank you to my publisher, Panta Press, and the incredible team of people working behind the scenes to help me share this important message with the world.

Foreword

I love to create, build, and grow. It's what excites me.

I've been an entrepreneur for over three decades, and my endeavors have spanned several industries such as music, beverages, private aviation, and self-improvement. And although those types of businesses may seem drastically different, the keys to my success were all very similar—daily habits, routines, and mindset.

Sometimes I've seen opportunities and taken them; other times I've created them out of thin air, and then on the rare occasion, I've been handed an opportunity. I think, in part, that's contributed to my success. Mostly, things haven't been given to me. I've had to figure everything out on my own, which has given me invaluable life and work experience, and I'm constantly learning.

Learning is paramount for every entrepreneur. It's like oxygen. Thankfully, there are so many different ways to acquire knowledge, especially in today's world. I'm a believer in experiential learning, but that sometimes comes at a cost—time and money. So we must continually look for ways to gain insight, gain an edge, and improve.

That's one of the reasons I love meeting new people—I never know what I might learn from a recent college grad after a public speaking event or a friend of a friend who wants five minutes of my time or even the guy asking for directions to Shake Shack. We never really know where the next bit of wisdom may come from, so with that in mind, I've been known to take a business meeting or two from time to time.

Okay, fine, I've taken a lot of business meetings.

I don't have a checklist or specific questions I always ask before investing in someone's company. But I always look into their eyes when they're sitting across from me and delivering their pitch. I want to see whether they have "it"—that undying hunger to succeed. And if I see "it" in their eyes, I often write a check. I'm investing in the person rather than the concept.

The other thing I look for is whether they have that entrepreneurial spirit.

Entrepreneurial spirit has been defined as a mindset. It's an attitude and approach to thinking that actively seeks out change, rather than waiting to adapt to change. It embraces critical questioning, innovation, service, and continuous improvement.

That perfectly describes Bonneau Ansley. He has "it" and the entrepreneurial spirit.

Everywhere I go, I see him. Well, I see photos of him on "For Sale" signs in big, beautiful front yards. And the name recognition is through the roof. Somehow, he's figured out how to have a bigger brand than anyone in the state. Do you remember the theory of six degrees of separation? It's the idea that all people are six, or fewer, social connections away from each other. Here in Atlanta, I bet we could play three degrees of Bonneau Ansley. He's not on the map—he is the map.

He's a first-rate entrepreneur and a top-selling real estate in Georgia. He's been recognized by the *Wall Street Journal* as one of the top real estate agents in the country. And, while his stat sheet is insanely impressive, he's done it all while also being a team player. He's constantly trying to teach, share, and lift others up. Fortunately, I've had a front-row seat to his incredible journey, which has been amazing and inspiring. And lucky for agents all around the world, he's sharing it all in *Brokering Billions*.

It doesn't matter where you're located, if growth is part of your business model, then this book will help you achieve your goals. His knowledge and wisdom transcend all boundaries and will provide amazing results. I believe his insight will help you think differently; it'll give you a new perspective that you didn't even realize you had, and it'll motivate you to create a bigger and better business.

Bonneau is an architect of paradigm shifts. He knows how to disrupt an industry and thrive. He has the unique ability to act decisively, and yet, he's willing to turn on a dime—he's comfortable with course correction. Equally impressive, he knows what he doesn't know, so he's always trying to improve and seeking advice from others to make informed decisions. But I think the most remarkable trait he has is that he's committed to the success of all.

I encourage you to keep this book handy on your desk.

—Jesse Itzler,
New York Times best-selling author and entrepreneur

Why I Wrote This Book

At fifteen years old, after years of struggling in school, I sold a batch of T-shirts and knew I was going to be okay. Despite my poor academic record and countless demerits, that sale helped me see a path toward some sort of success in life.

During the first fifteen years of my life, I did not fit in the one-size-fits-all box. No one knew what to do with me.

I had a few things I was good at. I could make people laugh. I was good at sports. And I could sell things. But academics weren't one of them.

Since then, as I have grown my business, I have learned that many successful people were just like me. They weren't good students but still became successful through working hard, working to their strengths, and building a mindset and structure that put them in the best position to do what they're good at and have other people do the things they don't do well.

I also learned that there were a lot of people who thought their "limitations" meant their ceiling in selling real estate was limited. Whether their perceived limitations were personal ("I'm not good at marketing" or "I'm not organized") or around them ("My market is small" or "There's a lot of competition in my market"), I've heard it all.

I also know all these perceived limitations can be overcome by putting in place a simple plan like I did. Not only have I used this process to sell billions of dollars in real estate but I've also helped hundreds of agents in my company and elsewhere elevate their business to new heights using the same process.

So while I continue to use what you'll learn in this book to scale my business, I want to help other agents do the same (especially those of you who, like me, had been told their whole life that they weren't good enough or smart enough to succeed in business).

As you'll learn about later in this book, as a young kid, when I was diagnosed with dyslexia and ADHD, the idea of becoming one of the top people in any profession seemed unreachable. But I wanted to show everyone that the dyslexic, ADHD misfit could not only succeed in business but could also help others do the same.

I wanted to show people that *anyone* can rise to the top with the right mindset, systems, and people in place.

I wanted to show people how to surround themselves with the right structure and support to allow them to do what they love and excel at, with the people, systems, and processes to take care of the rest.

And that's why I wrote this book.

I listed my first property in 2009. Since then, I have built one of the most successful real estate practices in the US. I have personally sold *billions* of dollars in residential real estate—more than $900 million between 2021 and 2022, each year earning me more than $25,000 *per day* in gross commissions. And starting from scratch in 2009 with just one listing, in a crowded market and during one of the worst real estate markets in history, I feel like I have a story to tell.

I built my business in a way that allows me to do what I love (and what I do better than anyone else). And I've helped hundreds of real estate agents do the same—putting systems and people in place to handle the pieces they don't do well (and don't enjoy doing) so they can focus on doing the pieces they're uniquely suited to excel at.

Now I want to help you do the same.

What you'll learn in this book is that success requires a combination of factors—many of which virtually nobody talks about. It requires systems. It requires people. And it requires work—hard work even. But you likely already know about that. A lot of people talk about that.

What few people talk about is that success also requires knowing yourself. You need to dig deep into your heart to understand what you really want in life. You need to understand what pieces of the puzzle you are uniquely qualified to perform. And you need to consistently strengthen your mindset—because the biggest obstacle you will face on the way to Brokering Billions™ is the one between your ears.

I believe that the greatest impact we can make on the world is not how successful we are in what we do and taking our secrets of success to the grave. Instead, I believe the greatest impact we can make is giving people the tools, resources, and confidence to achieve *their* vision of success in their lives.

I'm going to share the mindset, systems, team-building approach, and marketing strategies that can help *anyone* succeed because they are designed to help you focus on what you do well and love to do. Then have other people do the rest.

It's that simple.

I've even created additional resources for you at BrokeringBillions.com to help you implement these strategies.

If I can go from one listing in 2009 to personally selling more than $450 million in residential real estate in 2021 and more than $460 million in 2022, I know the sky's the limit for you too.

All you need to do is take action.

And the first step you need to take is to continue reading.

It's that simple.

Let's go.

Introduction

Meet the Dyslexic Broker with ADHD Who Sells Billions of Dollars of Real Estate and Still Makes It Home in Time for Dinner

I f you met me in high school, or even in college at the bar, or in 2009 when I first started selling real estate in Atlanta, Georgia, you probably would never have guessed that I would become the top real estate broker in the Southern US, consistently ranked among the top brokers in the entire country, selling hundreds of millions of dollars in real estate per year—and leading a company of more than four hundred agents growing their careers in a company I started from scratch.

As somebody who is dyslexic with severe ADHD, I was never seen as one of the "sharper" tools in the shed. And while I was able to turn my learning "disability" from a challenge to a superpower (stick around: we'll dive into this later), the odds were stacked against me in school and then again when I started selling real estate: I was about to enter a crowded market at the beginning of what would become the deepest economic downturn since the Great Depression.

I had just gone through the wringer—thanks to a disaster in the summer of 2004, which we'll get to in a bit—but things were finally looking up. The 2009 version of Bonneau was a hopeful man who had just started bouncing back.

I was in no shape to face *another* economic crisis. My hopes and dreams had been set up—yet again—to be crushed. I was excited about what I was doing, I was learning with each project, and I was making money. But that success was all for naught when Lehman Brothers collapsed in September 2008 and, with it, the entire real estate market.

It was such a bummer: I was having some great early success with different projects in Atlanta—a $100 million development in the middle of town. I also had ongoing developments on the South Carolina and Georgia coasts.

Sure enough, I ended up losing a lot of what I had worked for financially—along with so many friends and colleagues who lost a lot as well. But, as I just alluded to, the economic turmoil that came about in 2009 wasn't my first rodeo—I had experienced crushed dreams in the past. And, as you'll see, you can find your success in those curves . . .

A Three-Pronged Tip I Learned from One of My Mentors

My first real estate job was quite the doozy. I was working at the Ford Plantation, a luxury gated community just outside of Savannah, Georgia, trying to sell $500,000 lots to people as they came off the highway. When I was working there, the head broker, Peter Pollak, was an amazing mentor to me.

He taught me three sales techniques that had become completely habitual to him. But, to me, they were new. Early in my career, I learned to make them second nature, and they've since become invaluable to me—I still keep them in my bag of tricks. You can use them in any sales arena, not just real estate.

The first is **the art of the special situation**. For example, I often only had two or three hours max to get a potential client from off the highway to actually signing a contract. I would say, "God, I can't believe you're here today. You know, with everything you're telling me, you sound like you want to buy a wooded lot, on a lake, close to the golf clubhouse, where you can walk over with your clubs to hit balls. I have just the lot for you." In this way, I have created a special situation, one that is unique to this client and to that lot.

Next, I have to **create a sense of urgency**. People want a reason to buy, and you have to give them one. I would say, "You're not going to believe this, but yesterday, a guy signed a contract on this lot and is considering changing his mind to buy something on the river. This is the last lot next to the clubhouse. It's right on Lake Clara and has tons of beautiful trees on it." Now I have created a sense of urgency.

Finally, I have to **create a fear of loss**. "You better jump on this lot now because the other guy is driving in from Charleston tomorrow with his architect to look at things for a second time. So if you want the lot, I better put your name on it right now." The client then thinks, *This sounds like a great opportunity. I've always* *wanted to jump on opportunities like this and never have. This is what I need to do, you know?* In this way, you can get someone to sign on the dotted line fairly quickly, and they will be happy with their purchase for years to come.

Thanks to three sales techniques taught to me by my mentor, Peter Pollak, I outsold every other salesman on the property during my first year at the company.

If Your Mindset and Focus Aren't Aligning with Your Habits, Adjustments Are in Order

After borrowing these habits from Peter Pollak, my view at the Ford Plantation hadn't changed. I knew the development inside and out, and there were only a certain number of lots I could sell. I started to keep my ear to the ground and soon heard about a new development in Bluffton, South Carolina, on the May River, called Palmetto Bluff. Construction was just about to begin. It would be centered around a spectacular Auberge hotel, and I wanted in.

But my habits had changed. After I mastered those new habits, I drove to the new site and met with the head developer. I said, "Look, I want in on this project from a development standpoint." He looked at me like I was crazy. I wasn't even twenty-five years old yet, and I didn't have any development experience. But I talked my way in, through the sheer power of persuasion, to getting control of thirty lots around the future hotel when a shovel had yet to hit the ground.

I worked out some good terms with the developer, where I didn't have to put all of the money up front. I only paid a portion of the lot costs, and the developer held the note for the remaining lot price.

I agreed to pay that in full once construction was finished on the first lot and I sold the first house. I had my father cosign the loan with SunTrust Bank, which took some persuading, but he had just sold his business and I think he wanted to support my work as independent from him in the real estate industry. Though my father had been in real estate for years, I didn't have a family business to fall back on, which ended up being the best thing that's ever happened to me. My father's career had been much the same. He was a lawyer who struck out on his own with real estate when he got bored with private practice. He and his partner, Tom Bradbury, formed their company, Colony Homes, and sold close to two thousand homes in their best year. They were partners for nearly twenty-five years.

After I struck that deal with the developer, I then struck a deal with a builder I knew from the Ford Plantation, and we partnered up and started building in the core village, which surrounded the Auberge. The Village was the heartbeat of the development; the success of the whole project in many ways depended upon the success of the Village. The Village contained the marina, the docks, the sales office, a couple of restaurants and retail shops, and, almost most importantly, the post office. If anyone on this twenty thousand-acre development wanted to pick up their mail, they had to come to the Village. I had a gut instinct that it was the right place to be.

In the end, the builder and I ended up building over one hundred houses with an average price of $1 million, and we were wildly successful.

The point is that while old habits die hard, new habits can lift you to places you might not otherwise go, and every piece of the puzzle works in tandem with one another. Before I could take action with the right habits, I had to put together a plan. Before I could put together a plan, I had to have the right mindset.

I had a dream to sell dirt. I was obsessed with it. And I eventually put a plan into action through new habits to do just that—good old-fashioned shoe-leather hard work, day in and day out.

Your habits will either serve you or bring you down. As Vince Lombardi said, "Winning is a habit. Unfortunately, so is losing." The process of reverse engineering good habits will allow you to bypass those blockers that stand in your path. Only then can you make the shift, learn the lessons, and set the mark for your dreams and future goals. I'll talk all about the habits you need to Broker Billions in chapter 4. But first . . .

Let Me Take You Back to the Summer of 2004

My wife, Jen, and I were out to dinner one night in downtown Savannah, Georgia, where we lived. We were talking about our new baby, due only a month later. We were in our early twenties, having recently moved to Savannah together after graduating from the University of Georgia.

Jen was a quick, young real estate agent working for the best brokerage in town. At her high point, she had sixty listings. I was building homes and loving every day of work. The market was fantastic for both of us. We had a small group of loyal friends, some of whom were also expecting children of their own, and we loved spending weekends with them on the water, fishing in the mudflats and cooking out on the deck. Jen and I often talked about how fortunate we were, especially to have each other and to work in an industry we both loved and found fulfilling. We could see our life trajectory stretching out before us.

The Calm before the Storm

A year prior, we had just finished building our dream home. It sat at the end of a hammock island on the Wilmington River with views of the Savannah Yacht Club from our back porch. Historic Savannah, with all of its charm and culture, was just a short drive away. Occasionally, dolphins would swim right up to our dock. I was learning how to handle a boat and getting familiar with the waterways and sandbars, so much so the natives dubbed me "Sandy."

Both Jen and I love architecture, and it was a joy to work with our architect and designer to plan a home that we hoped would house our family for many years to come. It was exciting to watch the home being built from the ground up. With every house I've built before and since, I learn more, refine my eye, and marvel that a dwelling can rise, piece by piece, from raw dirt to become a home. After work in the evenings, Jen and I would often meet at the construction site to survey the progress and then grab a quick bite on the way home to our rental in Savannah.

Savannah is notorious for its hard and intense summer storms. That evening, there was a particularly hard storm, followed by a sunset of magical colors stretching over the marsh. As Jen and I crossed the causeway on the way back to our new home, we saw smoke starting to rise in the distance. It wasn't the kind of smoke you see from a brush fire burning in the country. This was black smoke. This was the kind of smoke you'd see when plastic, metal, and sheetrock were going up in flames. It was huge.

Soon, we began to smell the destruction. We knew that someone's life was going to change forever; we just didn't know it was our lives that were about to change. I instinctively started driving a little bit faster.

Everything Was Gone in a Flash

As we approached our neighborhood, we saw our neighbors out in the street—neighbors who had quickly become friends—looking in the direction of our car with blank stares. I will never forget how quiet it was. As we turned the corner, we saw what remained of our dream home, which had taken us two years to build.

That evening's storm had been so severe that lightning had struck our chimney and set the whole house in flames. The firemen had done everything they possibly could, but the blaze was too big. Our one consolation was that our Boykin spaniel, Bodie, whom we adored, was saved. The firemen found him cowering in a corner of the dining room and carried him out from the flames. Bodie lived to be seventeen, and you could always tell he had been through something. He was as reserved as he was gentle and kind.

Every aspect of our existence changed at that moment. We lost everything we'd ever owned. Our pictures from high school and college, family scrapbooks and mementos from generations before, wedding gifts from so many generous friends and family. We lost the nursery that we had so lovingly prepared for our baby; this room which in only a few weeks would have been filled with the smell and sounds of a newborn. We lost the guest room that was furnished with beds that were mine as a boy and my father's before me. At that moment, all Jen and I had were the clothes on our backs and each other.

A few days later, after we had caught our breath, we thanked the fire department and met with our insurance company, and then immediately turned to what was next. Our loss was so devastating we knew instinctively that we couldn't bear the pain of staying in Savannah. We decided to move home to Atlanta, where both of us had grown up and where our parents and extended families lived. We hardly looked back to our old life in Savannah and the rubble of our house we had left behind.

We moved into a rental house in Atlanta on a street where lots of friends lived and started to put the pieces of our life back together and regain a sense of normalcy. The next month, we welcomed our first child to the world—a girl we named Blakely, my mother's maiden name. After Blakely was born, we started to put the pieces of our life back together. We bought new furniture, plates, frying pans, a blender, a vacuum, underwear, sheets, you name it. Friends brought food to boost our spirits along with baby clothes, toys, a stroller, and a highchair for Blakely. Blakely was a happy, easy, healthy baby, keeping our spirits up and helping us with perspective and gratitude for all we had.

No matter how challenging that time was, Blakely's arrival and the love we felt from our friends reminded us that life was good.

What's Possible: Consistently Doubling Your Money

My family name was plastered all over town: on the country club, the high-end neighborhood Ansley Park, developed in 1904, and in many other corners of the city. Although my family had built a name in the city, I became obsessed with making my own mark and building my own success, independent of them.

Of course, that put a lot of pressure on me to succeed. But it was important to me to do so independently, so I made a point of starting from the bottom when I decided to get into selling residential real estate. I had no clients. I had no experience selling residential real estate in Atlanta. And I had one listing, a townhouse that was left over from my last development project.

But I was committed to being the top agent in Atlanta. So I focused on putting in place the people, processes, and tools that would lead to *fast*, consistent growth. I wanted to double my money and then double it again, and again, and again.

Fast forward twelve years, and I've been able to consistently do just that using the same mindset, systems, and strategies you'll learn in this book.

Of course, when you aim for growing fast and big, not everything goes well. I made a lot of mistakes—many of which were *expensive*. Despite that, though, I was still able to consistently double my growth. And what's here in this book is what worked best for me so you can learn from and avoid those mistakes. You'll make your own, of course. I still make mistakes. But if you keep going and doing what it takes to succeed, the future is bright.

Why Should You Read This Book?

From my beginnings selling houses, I committed to giving back to the real estate community in the form of sharing what I've learned, through mediums like this book. As the top broker in the Southeast US, I've faced my share of obstacles to get to where I am. I want to help you get to where I am while avoiding some of the struggles I faced building back.

That's why you're holding this book in your hands. In it, I will share the good, the bad, and the ugly of Brokering Billions. I'll share everything I've learned in going from selling my first house to earning tens of millions of dollars in commissions along the way.

I'll also introduce you to a dozen of the top real estate agents across the United States and share some of their stories about how they were able to achieve similar levels of success all across the country. Some of these real estate agents were mentors of mine early on. Others I met recently. But all of them are among the top real estate agents in the country. I'll briefly introduce you to each of them before we dive into all the details of Brokering Billions in chapter 1.

Most people mistakenly think obstacles are a drag on momentum. But the truth is that adversity forces you to develop successful habits. Every obstacle gives you the strength to face your next conflict. And that, practiced daily, is the real secret to doubling your business and improving your life.

If you have struggled to succeed, then we share something in common. If you have gotten knocked on your butt along the way, then we share something in common. And if you don't want to settle, and you want to constantly get better as a businessperson and an individual, then we share something in common.

I am here to tell you that these experiences and feelings are perfectly normal, and you should expect them as part of your path to growth. I will never forget the day I watched my house, and all my belongings, burn to the ground. It was a horrific experience. But what I didn't know then is that moment of adversity, of pure fear, started something big for me in my life.

That huge obstacle unlocked the opportunity for me to rise up and gradually climb from the bottom to the top. I welcomed a new beginning that day. That journey has brought me to writing this book, a guide of sorts to help you build something meaningful, exciting, and supercharged in your own life.

Let Me Show You the Way

When I was presented with obstacles, I remained driven. I was committed to doing whatever I needed to do to succeed. That said, there was one caveat: I would never sacrifice my family to build my business. I had seen way too many people throw away marriages, relationships with kids, and even their health in a relentless pursuit of "more."

Nonetheless, I became obsessed with my success, entering a market already packed with nineteen thousand agents and brokers. If you had to bet, you'd be more likely to put your money on me flaming out within a matter of months than rising to the top of the market. Yet here I am, just a little over a decade later, killing it.

These days, I take things in stride; the strife I've faced in the past is but a testament to perseverance and nothing more. I've learned the ins and outs of the industry, and I've wised-up. Now, I'm writing this book to impart the lessons I've learned so I can help brokers like you avoid making the same mistakes. My goal is to help agents like you hit goals that are even bigger than they dreamed, like the goals I had hit by the time I wrote this book for you:

- Achieved $900+ million personal volume in 2021 and 2022
- Achieved over $10 million gross commission in 2021 and 2022
- Led a company that did over $3 billion in annual sales
- Became the youngest in Georgia to hit $1 billion in sales
- Was named Number One Agent in the South, per the *Wall Street Journal*
- And, most importantly, still came home every night by 6:00 p.m. and didn't work weekends

Although I have achieved a lot of big goals, it wasn't all smooth sailing. In the early days, I faced tons of trial and error. There was a lot of pivoting, recalibrating, and falling flat on my face before I started to achieve more regular success. Yet, despite those struggles, I was still able to grow my business exponentially. Why is that important? Because it means you don't have to be perfect to Broker Billions.

I learned the ropes the hard way; I was eating dust before I was crushing my competition. Obstacles stopped me in my tracks time and time again, giving me harsh reality checks, and I learned quickly that getting to the top wouldn't happen if I let any of those reality checks stop me.

The lessons I've learned along the way have proved invaluable for countless brokers just like you. They've helped me to overcome obstacles and eventually get to where I currently am. The reason I'm writing this book is to help brokers like you implement the same proven tactics I used to rise to the top of the real estate market.

A Day in the Life of a Top Broker

As I'll explain later in the book, the differences between an average broker and a top broker are simple and subtle. That said, the impact of those simple and subtle differences on your life is incredible. Aside from the obvious income benefits, your workdays become easier, more enjoyable, and (importantly) shorter.

Take my typical day, for example. From the outside, a typical day for Team Bonneau might even look uneventful. It usually starts with me getting a call on my cell, typically a referral through a past client from the last decade.

And they'll say, "Hey, you sold Joe Jones's house on West Wesley Road, and we've been getting your postcards for years. We've been following your success, and we'd like you to come look at our house. We are thinking about downsizing. We've got a second home and the kids are grown. When can you meet?"

We schedule a time, even as early as that afternoon, and then I immediately send the information to my team so they can get to work. Our listing coordinator, who is in charge of engaging with sellers, starts preparing the listing paperwork and then pulls up the surrounding sales in the neighborhood. My core team member, Hil Harper (who you'll meet later), reviews and blesses the information and then enters it into comparative market analysis.

Before my meeting, the listing coordinator will drop the comparative market analysis, the *Ansley Collection* book, and the listing agreement at the client's house, all in a beautiful proprietary silver box with an Ansley logo on the side. A couple of hours before I show up at the home, we send our listing presentation to the potential seller digitally. Hopefully, the potential seller will recognize how professional our materials are, as well as understand where we stand on commission rates. I always take a team member with me to the interview so the client can understand how the team works and can meet another team member.

We begin by touring the house. I always make sure I compliment several features of the house to show my respect—like, "Hey, I love the floor in the entrance hall." I talk a bit about my knowledge of the neighborhood and then try to find that connection with the potential client to help me stand out from the other agents they might be interviewing.

Next, I will go through the contract with them and give them a strategy to sell their house: a list price, a probable sales price, and a thirty-, sixty-, and ninety-day marketing plan. I also tell them that

I have scheduled photos of their house to be taken in two days, confident that I already have the job. I then detail everything we need to do to maximize the home's value and make sure it sells fast, such as staging, pre-listing inspections, and my list of "must-do" prep work to make sure the home is in the best selling condition prior to showing it, such as spreading new pine straw outdoors, putting fresh flowers on the coffee table, cleaning gutters and windows, getting current on any pest treatments, and ensuring the pool is in good repair.

"Don't worry," I emphasize to the seller, making sure they know working with me is a no-stress relationship. "We have qualified partners in every one of these areas who know exactly what to do to maximize your property's value. You don't need to do anything."

Once the client has signed the contract, our listing coordinator orders the yard sign, perhaps meets our stager at the house to get it ready for the home photos, and takes care of any other further details that might need to be tended to before showings, such as gutter cleaning, pressure washing, reorganizing closets, or painting. Then she meets the photographer onsite to take the photos. After we receive the raw photographs, she works directly with our marketing department to design the home brochure, schedule the social media posts, and do anything else we might need to do related to this home and its marketing.

Before listing the property in the MLS (if you're new to real estate, that stands for Multiple Listing Services), however, we conduct multiple pre-listing marketing campaigns, including a "coming soon" marketing campaign as well as internal company announcements. (More on these in chapter 8). If we don't get a buyer for the property using pre-listing campaigns, we activate the listing on the MLS.

Once we list the house on the MLS, the phone starts ringing, and we start scheduling showings. I've taken this scheduling component out of my day because going back and forth trying to work with multiple people's schedules was taking time away from what I do best. It's part of freeing me up to do what I do best.

On our thirty-day marketing plan, we'll typically schedule an open house on a Sunday and a "caravan" on a Tuesday where we invite the Atlanta real estate community for a nice pickup lunch and viewing between 11:30 a.m. and 2 p.m.

Hopefully, we will get a good offer within the first thirty days. At that time, the team member who is the lead for that property starts negotiating the contract with our listing clients. Any changes to the contract will be done by our closing coordinator.

Once we have a signed deal, the closing coordinator makes sure we collect earnest money at the right time, that it's deposited in the right place, and that there's communication between the closing attorney and the buyer and seller of the transaction. She ensures we progress and notate contract negotiations, dates relative to appraisals and financing contingencies, due diligence, and inspection-related questions. Then I will typically be the one who goes to the closing and handles the settlement charges. Hopefully, we'll get a great Zillow review and ask for the next referral.

Although that might not seem tremendously different from what many real estate agents or brokers do, each element of the process is carefully designed to separate me and my team from the approximately two million real estate agents in the United States as of the time I write. All of these details have helped me become the number one broker in Atlanta.

What to Expect: Brutal Honesty

Let me set a few expectations from the start.

First, I'm going to share the unfiltered truth about what it takes to become one of the top real estate brokers in your area (or even the entire country). As you'll learn, it doesn't take long hours or some complex marketing system to get started. In fact, it will likely appear refreshingly simple. But what it *does* take is consistency and a commitment to get out of your comfort zone for a little while as you build your momentum.

Second, I'm going to share the highs and the lows of Brokering Billions. While the numbers I shared already might seem exciting, Brokering Billions is not without its challenges, especially as you grow. Nobody's business is a straight shot up from average to the top—we all hit obstacles and setbacks. But what you do along the way and how you react when adversity strikes are what will lead to the results you achieve. It doesn't matter who you are or what you've done: if you face adversity with determination, you can get the results you want.

If you hit adversity and back off, your business will suffer. Your progress will stall. You could move backward, even. But if you hit adversity and push forward—even when it's uncomfortable to do so—your business will benefit in the long run.

Third, I'm going to show you where and how to invest in your business for long-term growth and success. If you focus on short-term benefits at the expense of the long term, you could end up in a world of hurt. But if you focus on the long term and building a solid business and foundation, your setbacks and obstacles won't cause you to collapse.

I'm going to walk you through exactly how to build the foundation and then get into the mindset and actions you need to take to be successful. And I'm going to introduce you to others who are Brokering Billions all over the United States, in cities and suburban areas, in highly competitive areas, and everywhere in between. You'll be learning from the best of the best, as I'll be offering insight from fellow billion-dollar brokers.

In the next part of the book, we'll set the foundational pieces to Brokering Billions. Way too many people skip these foundational steps and go straight to marketing thinking all they need to do to succeed is get more people to know about them. While that's helpful—after all, it doesn't matter how good you are if nobody knows you exist—the *worst* thing you can do is market a business that isn't ready for prime time. Marketing is important—*critical* even—but, as a friend of mine says, "If your business sucks, why would you want more people to know about it?"

It's true. You need to always be marketing your business. But you need to make sure your business is worth marketing and won't collapse from the business your marketing brings in. I'll talk about how to market your business. But before I do, it's time to make sure you build a billion-dollar foundation.

The Agent of the Future

"If you always do what you've always done, you always get what you've always gotten."

— Jessie Porter

Before we get started helping you Broker Billions, we need to talk about "conventional wisdom." This won't be the last time we talk about conventional wisdom in the book, but it's important enough that I want to highlight it up front because if there's one piece of advice I could give new agents or agents who are struggling, it's to ignore conventional wisdom and instead focus on becoming the agent of the future.

One surefire way to tell whether you're effectively ignoring conventional wisdom is to get in the room with some of the old guard and see how they treat you. If they treat you as one of them, you might be in trouble. If they tell you you're crazy or say you're not doing things the right way, you might just be onto something big. And, if you apply what you're going to learn over the rest of this book, you'll *definitely* be onto something big.

There's probably no better example than Ryan Serhant's experience at The Real Deal's NYC Showcase + Forum on May 19, 2022. For those of you who don't know Ryan, he's the CEO of SERHANT., which he also founded about twenty months before the forum after only getting started selling real estate in 2008, just one year before I started selling real estate in Atlanta.

Why? Two reasons.

1. Like me, *his results exceeded his relative influence, budget, and experience in the market.* I was the top-producing agent in all of Atlanta my first year selling real estate there. This was among thousands of agents and dozens, if not hundreds, of brokerage firms who started the year with more brand recognition, experience, and money than I did. In my case, I was able to outsell all the agents at those companies by doing things differently.

2. *The only way to stand out of the crowd in an industry with thousands of people is to be different.* And people like Serhant, me, and other agents I'm going to introduce you to in this book have all been able to stand out over a long period, with each of us selling hundreds of millions of dollars in real estate a year and billions of dollars overall.

Unsurprisingly, Serhant's experience at The Real Deal's event was mixed, so much so that he recorded a five-minute response on Instagram detailing what happened and addressing some of the negative comments he received about having been the product of reality TV and social media. In his words:

"Everyone is entitled to their own opinions on reality TV. Obviously, some of it's trash. Some of it's actually amazing. But what reality TV for real estate has done is it's brought the business to millions of people who otherwise might not have been interested in it. I mean, look at HGTV. Look at the Property Brothers. Do you think the fact that the Property Brothers were able to renovate a full house and have fun with it and do it in 22 minutes has hurt the general contracting business? No."

This is important. Conventional wisdom suggests that you sell real estate through the things listed on the legacy company websites—things like information, service, and professionalism. The truth is all those things are the cost of entry. People *assume* you have access to information, provide quality service, and will be a professional. Those things don't help you stand out. In other words, if information, service, and professionalism are your lead value offers, people won't be impressed.

Serhant continued, noting what real estate reality TV did for the real estate billions was to expose the idea of upgrading homes, owning multiple properties, and owning investment properties to millions of people. Many of these people might never have thought about flipping homes, buying rental properties, or wanting larger homes with features they'd never seen before had it not been for reality TV.

In his words, real estate reality TV "has made the business of being a real estate agent more diverse, made it more open to more groups of people, and made it something that younger people would actually want to do when they graduate high school or graduate college. And it's been really, really amazing for our industry, whether you like the specific shows or not."

And while I'm not necessarily suggesting you start or join the cast of a reality TV show, I do want to encourage you to think differently than the old guard.

Don't aim to be the agent of the past but the agent of the future who sells homes because you use technology, social media, and every other creative resource at your disposal to get eyeballs on you and even more eyeballs on the properties you sell. Because, when people want to hire a real estate agent, they really only care about two numbers: how much can I get for my house and how fast can you sell it.

To help your clients get full value for their homes and sell them fast, it doesn't matter how long you've been in business. It took me less than one year to be the top agent in Atlanta, and I've been able to consistently stay on top by constantly staying ahead of the old guard, despite their bigger budgets and decades longer of experience.

How? Because I built my agency for the future. As they say in hockey, I don't skate toward the puck, I skate where it's going. That's how I Broker Billions.

I hope you're ready. This is going to be a lot of fun—and *very* profitable.

The Other Billion-Dollar Brokers Who Agreed to Help You Broker Billions

When writing a book like this, the natural tendency for an author is to only share stories, systems, and strategies that are straight out of their personal experiences. However, as you'll hear a few times in this book, one of the most important things you can do to Broker Billions is to surround yourself with mentors, peers, and others outside of the real estate world to learn from, share experiences with, and build mutually beneficial relationships.

Thus, it would be completely inconsistent with how I built my business and what I recommend for you if this book were all about me. So I decided to interview some of the smartest, most successful real estate entrepreneurs in the country to share their stories and advice with you too.

I have business and personal relationships with each of these people. Some were mentors of mine early on. Others work with me today in various capacities, including partners, agents at my company, referral relationships, and more. They're all rock stars in their areas whose paths to success demonstrate the principles I'll share with you throughout this book.

Before we get into the content, I wanted to briefly introduce you to them.

Thad Wong

Thad Wong has built a career based on one foundational principle: "relationship is everything." He took that approach with @ properties, which he cofounded with his partner Mike Golden in 2000, and he continues to take that approach with everything he does today. He and Mike have grown @properties to the nation's eighth largest brokerage firm by sales volume, per RealTrends 500. @properties and its affiliated companies boast more than 3,500 agents in thirteen states with annual closed sales volume of more than $16 billion.

In 2021, @properties expanded its impact and presence by purchasing Christie's International Real Estate and Thad became co-CEO with Mike Golden.

When Christie's International Real Estate and @properties announced the deal, Christie's International Real Estate's chief operating officer, Ben Gore noted that the company chose to enter into the transaction, in part, "because @properties possesses the unique resources and capabilities to invest in expanding the Christie's International Real Estate brand and its affiliate network both within the US and on a global scale."

That's high praise coming from the chief operating officer of such a well-known global brand. And it's well deserved. Thad is one of the most capable, strategic, and innovative brokers in the world. He's built one of the most advanced marketing and operational real estate technology platforms in the world. And he's helped thousands of agents maximize their impact by giving them all the technology and other tools and support they need so they can focus on what they do best: building relationships and selling homes.

Mark Spain

In 2011, after fifteen years of practicing real estate, Mark Spain joined Keller Williams and formed the Mark Spain Team. Over the next five years, the Mark Spain Team helped over 3,500 families close on their homes. In 2016, Mark Spain announced independence from Keller Williams and formed Mark Spain Real Estate. In 2021, his team sold more than $3.3 billion in residential real estate and served more than 10,300 clients. Mark Spain Real Estate was also named the number one real estate team for closed transactions in the US for five consecutive years by the *Wall Street Journal*.

He has also been a mentor to me for the past thirty years, having first met him in the sales trailer as a teenager when he was working for my father at Colony Homes. I've been fortunate to be able to learn from and live life with Mark for decades.

Glennda Baker

In residential sales and marketing for nearly twenty-six years, Glennda Baker specializes in the purchase and sale of Atlanta homes and properties in the surrounding area for Ansley | Christie's International Real Estate, having sold $70 million in real estate in 2021.

Glennda is known as the number one real estate agent on TikTok, having amassed close to one million followers between TikTok and Instagram in less than three years, earning her approximately 2.5 million views per week across her video catalog.

The Ussery Group

Johnny Ussery, Keene Reese, and their team and partners have been a part of many of the master-planned communities in Hilton Head-Bluffton since Johnny's arrival in the area in 1980.

Together, they are the number one real estate company in the Lowcountry, with eleven offices located throughout the Hilton Head-Bluffton area.

At the Ussery Group, Johnny, Keene, and their partners practice "real estate the right way" and hold one another to the highest standards of integrity. Collectively, they've sold over a billion dollars of real estate—and they've done it the right way.

Holly Parker

A real estate industry powerhouse with well over $8 billion in sales, Holly consistently achieves annual sales of over $500 million and has been repeatedly honored with Douglas Elliman's most prestigious sales awards. Holly consistently outperforms sales projections, setting records and making her developers and sellers incredibly happy.

An experienced real estate investor, she has a firsthand understanding of today's market challenges and can walk clients through the real estate process from start to finish with confidence and finesse. Buyers and sellers alike will benefit from Holly's honest and straightforward approach to real estate investment analysis and her creative financial consultation.

Jonathan Spears

Jonathan has always considered himself an overachiever—someone who is unwilling to settle for the status quo. His exceptional drive was evident even as a teenager when he enrolled in college before he could legally drive a car. Desiring to develop a greater understanding of the business side of the real estate profession, Jonathan opted to focus his studies at Florida State University on business and finance, graduating with a degree in business administration at nineteen years old.

Coupled with his natural entrepreneurial spirit, Jonathan discovered an opportunity to parlay his degree with his desire to launch a career in real estate when he started off working in the foreclosure resale business in his hometown of Destin, Florida. In 2015, Jonathan joined Scenic Sotheby's International Realty. Utilizing his "go-getter" attitude and superior knowledge of the northwest Florida real estate market, Jonathan rapidly developed a stranglehold on the luxury real estate market in the area.

With business booming after only two short years, Jonathan began assembling a talented team of his own that would operate under the Scenic Sotheby's International Realty brand; thus, Spears Group was formed. In 2020, Jonathan and his team closed over $265 million in sales, and for the second consecutive year, Jonathan was named the youngest member of "The Thousand Top Real Estate Professionals," as published in the *Wall Street Journal*—inking him in the top one-half of 1 percent of the more than 1.3 million Realtors® nationwide by individual sales volume.

Julie Faupel

In addition to being a top-producing real estate professional, Julie is the founder and CEO of REALM, the most elite membership of real estate professionals ever assembled. REALM involvement is by invitation only and includes a patented technology platform that enriches individual client data while activating the databases of the membership in a completely anonymized manner. Julie's career path before real estate includes twelve years of management and consulting experience for luxury hotels and small businesses.

In 2021, she sold sixty homes and closed $327 million in sales in the white-hot, high-end Jackson Hole, Wyoming, market.

Rob Thomson

Rob Thomson is the owner of Waterfront Properties in Jupiter, Florida, providing industry-leading service to clients across southern Florida. With over eighty expert agents across five offices in Palm Beach and Martin counties, no matter what a client is looking for in the luxury property market, Waterfront has the professionals to provide the best information, guidance, and support.

From innovative digital and traditional marketing techniques to resources that span across the globe, Waterfront Properties has the tools that put it on top of the luxury property market. One key to Rob Thomson and Waterfront Properties' success is the proprietary, award-winning technology and innovation-based marketing systems plus many other resources he and his agents have at their disposal. In 2021, Rob hit $445 million in sales.

Leigh Marcus

Leigh Marcus has sold over 2,000 properties since beginning his real estate career in Chicago approximately fifteen years ago. A real estate broker with @properties specializing in single-family homes and condos on Chicago's North Side, Leigh works with everyone from first-time home buyers and sellers to luxury clients.

Before joining the industry, Marcus worked in technology sales at IBM, CDW, and EMC for fifteen years. In 2019, Marcus represented the listing that garnered the highest transaction in Roscoe Village in over a decade. He has been recognized as a top producer by the Chicago Association of REALTORS® for five years straight and has even made the Inc. 5000 list multiple times. In 2021 alone, he sold 329 units, representing approximately $230 million in properties.

Josh Anderson

Originally from Nashville, Josh graduated from Louisiana State University with a degree in international trade and finance. Josh served eight years in the US Army, including a ten-month stint in Bagram, Afghanistan, during Operation Enduring Freedom.

Josh is a focused, disciplined, and strong-willed individual with high energy and a passion for Nashville real estate. In 2021, Josh Anderson completed 259 transactions totaling about $135 million in volume with a team of seven people supporting him.

Elizabeth DeWoody

In just six years, Elizabeth DeWoody went from selling her first home for a relative to selling more than $250 million in 2021 alone. She's an individual agent with a support staff born, raised, and working in southern Florida.

Before getting into real estate, she was a stay-at-home mom for several years, taking time to spend with her kids after working in marketing for Procter & Gamble and Johnson & Johnson for several years.

Chapter 1:

Casting Your Vision for the Business and Life You Want

There's never been a better time to enter the real estate market. This is true no matter what the local real estate market looks like because there's more wealth in the world than ever before, and agents who do what top brokers in the country do will be fine in any market.

In hot markets, you benefit from market conditions, but competition for listings is fierce. In cold markets, fewer homes might come on the market, but competition for listings can be lower, because of average agents not being able to stand out or land listings and having to leave the industry.

No matter what the market looks like, however, people need help from good agents. They know we more than make up for our commissions by selling their houses faster, for better prices, and with a greater ability to make sure deals close than if they tried to sell their home by owner. And buyers need help, expertise, and connections too.

Hot market, cool market, it doesn't matter. Seller's market or buyer's market, it doesn't matter. People need help. They're either going to get help from you or someone else. If you want it to be you, you *need* to be the best of the best and to make sure people know you exist and that you're the only person they should work with if they want to achieve their goals. You don't build that reputation by accident. And you don't build that reputation alone. But the good news is you don't need to be some super focused, workaholic, 4.0 GPA superhuman to build that reputation.

All you need to do is put in place the simple systems, people, and processes that let you work to your strengths while other people handle what you don't want or need to do.

When you do, you can truly get everything you want from this profession and make more money than ever while doing the tasks you enjoy and are good at. That's what I built, and I didn't have the benefit of a book like this to tell me how to do it. I had to figure it out on my own. If I could do it, so can you—especially with the benefit of learning from my mistakes.

The first step in building a business and life you love is to make sure you're working toward *your* best life, performing the tasks *you* love to do and are good at in your work. That's why I put together what I call the "Brokering Billions Blueprint" to have you cast your vision for what you're looking to build and then follow a simple process to help you achieve your specific goals. That's what we'll do right now.

Writing the Final Scene of Your Life Story

If you're struggling to even dream of a better life right now, try this exercise. Momentarily step out of your world and pretend you're writing a movie. The movie is about an agent just like you. At the beginning of the movie, their life is just like yours. In the end, they're still selling homes, but they *love* their life. I don't just mean *love*. They LOVE it. They love what they do during the day. They love their hours. They love their lifestyle. They love everything about their life.

Don't worry about the middle of the movie just yet—how they got from where they are today to where they want to be. I'll help you write that part over the rest of the book. That's the Brokering Billions Blueprint.

For now, take a minute to write the final scene. The "Happily Ever After" scene. Where does the agent in the movie live? What do they do all day? With whom do they spend the most time? When you're done writing down what the final scene would look like, replace this hypothetical agent with you.

For example, you might start with something like the below and then substitute yourself in place of the fictional character living your dream life:

"She lives on a quiet street with her husband, two kids, and a dog. Her husband stays home with the kids and helps her with some of her listings while the kids are in school. She is in the best shape of her life, meeting most of her new clients at the gym or tennis club. She spends most of her days networking at the gym, tennis club, or local restaurants. She loves working with people but is terrible with details, so she has a team that takes care of all the details to make sure everything goes smoothly with clients.

"She balances work and home well, coaching both of her kids' soccer teams without ever missing a practice or game. On the summer weekends, she takes the family to a lakefront property where they swim, hike, and fish. Every winter, they take a ski trip to Vail. Although she's willing to take a few phone calls while away if needed, she rarely hears from the office."

Think about your movie. How would it end? Would your last scene show an overworked real estate broker who lives at the whim of overbearing clients? Would you be working 120 hours a week? Would nothing work in your business unless you were involved?

Or would you work much less, have complete control over your schedule, work with clients who value you, and be able to enjoy both your business and personal life? And, of whatever hours you work, would you be focusing on the pieces you love to do, or would you be doing the work you hate? (If you need help figuring out what parts of the process you enjoy, go to BrokeringBillions. com/Quiz to identify the best fit for you.)

The Dangers of Dreaming Too Small

> *"The greater danger for most of us lies not in setting our aim too high and falling short; but in setting our aim too low, and achieving our mark."*
> —Michelangelo

When I talk with brokers, one of the most common impressions I get is that people are dreaming too small. They think one step ahead of where they are, maybe two or three at best. For example, if someone's selling $1 million in real estate, they dream of getting to $5 million or $10 million. Rarely would that person dream of selling $100 million or even $250 million.

So aim big. Really big, as if *anything* is possible. This is the final scene of the movie about your life, and you get to write it. What ending would you want to see before you walk out of the theater?

Ignore Your Competition

Another common impression I observe with brokers who struggle to rise to the top is that many people set their vision based on what their competition is doing. When their competitors are reaching $10 million in sales, they set their ceiling at $5 million, $10 million, or even $15 million.

While understandable, your competition should be irrelevant to what you pursue. Their results are based on the actions they took, the vision they cast, and the foundation they built. And, if they're like most average or even above-average brokers, they likely didn't do much planning. They likely followed conventional wisdom or the advice of their first mentor or boss instead of casting their own vision and then designing the people, systems, and processes to help them achieve it.

You have a choice. You can either follow conventional wisdom or in the footsteps of someone who likely followed it, or you can do what *the* most successful brokers in the industry did to rise to the top.

If you directly or indirectly follow conventional wisdom, you'll be pointed straight toward becoming an average agent. If that's what you want, I can't help you.

If you do what the most successful brokers did, then you'll cast a big vision for your business and your life and then take action to turn that vision into your reality. If that's what you want, I'm your man.

To Broker Billions, you need to forget about the competition. Forget about the broker who has been working in your community for thirty years. Forget about the agent who says they've tried "everything" to stand out but "nothing works." I'm going to help you make them irrelevant anyway.

Make the Destination Worth the Journey

When working toward anything new, important, and big, one thing is certain: You *will* struggle. You *will* face obstacles. You *will* stumble. You *will* have moments when you want to quit.

I did. I still do because I'm constantly adjusting my dreams, casting a bigger and bigger vision for my business and life.

What I've learned along the way is that when the goal you're aiming for is small, you're much more likely to quit when things get tough. For example, how much struggle would you be willing to endure to receive an additional $25,000 in gross commissions and a weekend off twelve years from now? Probably some but not *that* much. Now, how much struggle would you be willing to endure for over $25,000 in gross commissions *a day* with *every* weekend off twelve years from now—only doing minimal work on weekends that doesn't interrupt your dream life? Probably more. Much more.

If those numbers seem too specific to be made up, it's because they're not. Twelve years after I got my first listing, I averaged over $25,000 in gross commissions *a day* while making it home for dinner most nights and not being tied to my business on the weekends.

It wasn't a straight shot to the top. I didn't avoid struggle. I didn't avoid stumbling. I made *a lot* of mistakes. But I was pursuing something so important to me that it was worth all the struggles: becoming the top agent around while still being present with my family. I'm actually grateful to make some mistakes to build a life and business like that.

The same will be true for you. You'll be able to learn from my mistakes; you'll make your own mistakes too. But if you set your sights on a small goal, there's no way you'll push through your struggles. It won't be worth it. Make your destination worth the journey.

I'm not alone either. Take Holly Parker, for example, whom I interviewed for this book to share some of *her* story about how she brokers billions. Holly is the founder and CEO of Holly Parker Team, a real estate group that has sold more than $8 billion in real estate. She personally sold $386 million in sales in 2021 alone. Did I mention that Holly works in the New York City market? Talk about *competitive*. But it doesn't matter. With the right mindset, systems, and people in place, you can stand out anywhere, just like Holly does in New York City.

Holly is also the author of *Back on the Market: A Realtor's Guide to Love and Life* (Forefront Books, 2020), which takes you inside her life after divorce, connecting love and life with common real estate terms.

But Holly wasn't always Brokering Billions. In fact, if not for the advice of an early mentor, Holly might never have started selling real estate. Specifically, while working for a company helping relocate executives from Boston to London, someone encouraged her to interview everyone her family knows about their work. In doing so, she interviewed several real estate brokers and observed that they seemed to live a pretty flexible lifestyle.

"I noticed that they could just grind when they wanted to grind and took time off and traveled when they needed to catch their breath," Holly recalls. "I really liked that aspect of things and, at twenty-two years old, felt really lucky to have learned that lesson. I knew I wanted a big life, a life of adventure. And I learned that selling real estate certainly gives you that flexibility."

From the beginning, Holly knew exactly what she wanted for her life. She knew the destination she was heading toward, and it was big and important—a life of travel, flexibility, and adventure. I have no doubt that big vision helped push Holly through many obstacles over the years.

Appreciate the Struggle

In mid-2022, a video clip went viral of a man giving a speech about struggle. The clip doesn't reveal who is speaking or who the speaker is quoting, and it was shared by thousands of people, so the original source of the quote is unclear. However, the impact and purpose of the story remain, no matter who the original source may be:

"My grandfather walked ten miles to work every day. My father walked five. I'm driving a Cadillac. My son is in a Mercedes. My grandson will be in a Ferrari. My great grandson will be walking again. So I asked him, 'Well, why is that?' And he said to me, 'Tough times create strong men. Strong men create easy times. Easy times create weak men. Weak men create tough times.'"

If you want to see the clip for yourself, you can find it on the resources page at BrokeringBillions.com.

Although I'm not going to intentionally create tough times for you—quite the opposite, actually—with anything new, you will struggle. But those struggles will build strength. They'll teach you lessons. They'll help you achieve real, sustainable success, as long as you push through the adversity and keep going.

Thad Wong: From Dream to Dream Company

Thad Wong met his now-partner, Mike Golden, in 1996 at a small brokerage firm in downtown Chicago owned by a real estate developer. Although he and Mike would officially become partners in 1997, they kept their numbers separate so they would always be numbers one and two in the city. Sometimes Mike was one and Thad was two. Other years, Thad was one and Mike was two.

A few years later, Thad and Mike were approached by a developer client who didn't want to work with agents who worked under the umbrella of their competitor's brokerage firm. If they wanted to avoid losing that developer's business, they had a choice: open their own firm or go to a different brokerage.

In the face of an ultimatum, Thad and Mike sat down to envision what they might want to build together if they decided to open their own firm. They recalled how underappreciated they felt at their company. They were responsible for a large percentage of revenue but felt like they were putting in much more than they were getting out of the company. They were developing all their own materials and everything they needed to grow their business.

So they started wondering what it might look like if they opened their own firm that took an agent-first approach. They listed all the things agents were typically good at and thought they could build a company that provided all things agents typically struggled with, such as greater consistency, marketing assistance, organizational support and infrastructure, and content.

Ultimately, they decided to put all their efforts into building an agency just like that and that's how @properties was born. For the first few years, Thad and Mike aggressively sold to help the company get off the ground. Then, as the company got its wings, they put the most effort into growing the business.

As agents joined, they quickly became committed to the company, plugging into the @properties infrastructure and technology. They knew Thad and Mike were working in their best interests to grow their businesses and had designed the business for agents to get more out of the business than they put in. And they knew that the more they put into the business, the more they could get out.

Now twenty-two years later, Thad describes the business as pretty much the same, only bigger. "Nothing's really different, twenty-two years later," he says. "It's the same thesis—that the agents get a lot more being in the company than they put in. In the real estate world, that's not always the case. Oftentimes, agents feel like they pay the company more than what they get from the company. I always want the agent to feel like it's fair. I want them to feel like they pay the company a fair amount for what they are able to get back, and get even more back from the company than they put in."

Thad also emphasized that agents at @properties have trust and confidence that the company has a plan to unveil even more products, tools, and points of differentiation that help them become number one in their market faster.

Today, @properties and its affiliated companies have more than 3,500 agents in thirteen states, with annual closed sales volume of more than $16 billion.

And it all started with a vision.

It's Time to Dream

In the next chapter, I'm going to help you develop what I call a "Billion-Dollar Mindset." For our purposes, a Billion-Dollar Mindset is simply the mindset needed to Broker Billions while living a life you love—whatever that means to you.

Before we turn the page to the next chapter, take a few minutes to sit down in your director's chair and complete the first draft of the final scene of the movie about your life.

Where are you living? What do you do all day? What parts of the home selling process do you handle? What parts are handled by others? How do you meet clients? How long do you work? Be as specific as possible and don't worry about it being perfect. You can always edit it later. But take a few minutes to dream big about the life you would live if anything were possible.

Chapter 2:

Developing a Billion-Dollar Mindset

"Here's to the crazy ones. The misfits. The rebels. The troublemakers. The round pegs in the square holes. The ones who see things differently. They're not fond of rules. And they have no respect for the status quo. You can quote them, disagree with them, glorify or vilify them. About the only thing you can't do is ignore them. Because they change things. They push the human race forward. And while some may see them as the crazy ones, we see genius. Because the people who are crazy enough to think they can change the world, are the ones who do."

—Rob Siltanen

I f you came across my friend Jesse Itzler today, you might assume he has always been a high achiever. After all, straight out of college, he signed a recording contract as a songwriter and artist, eventually hitting the Billboard Hot 100 chart. He also cowrote songs for many people, including rapper Tone Lōc.

If that wasn't enough, just five years after his debut album, he cofounded his own record company. Five years after that, he cofounded Marquis Jet, a private jet card company, serving as the company's vice chairman until it was sold to Warren Buffett's Berkshire Hathaway.

He has since written two best-selling books, *Living with a SEAL: 31 Days Training With the Toughest Man on the Planet* (Center Street, 2015) and *Living with the Monks: What Turning Off My Phone Taught Me about Happiness, Gratitude, and Focus* (Center Street, 2018). He's become an ultra-endurance athlete, completing an Ultraman, (6.2-mile open water swim, 261.4-mile bike, 52.4-mile run) at the age of fifty-three. He and his wife, Sara Blakely, founder of Spanx, are also part owners of the Atlanta Hawks.

Needless to say, he's a pretty successful and motivated guy. But if you ask Jesse about how (and why) he does so many hard things, his answer might surprise you. "I like to push myself," Jesse admits. "But, for me, it wasn't always like that. I started out with a goal of running two miles in a day. That was my goal. If I could run for eighteen minutes, nine-minute miles, for two miles, I was a runner. But I was able to take that two-mile body and complete a one hundred-mile race. What's amazing and interesting is that my body really didn't change from when I started running and when I completed my first one hundred-mile run. I still had the same legs I was born with. I wasn't super strong.

"But my mind changed. Through doing things that were really hard consistently—every day pushing myself—my mind changed enough to enable the same legs that struggled to run two miles in a row to complete a one hundred-mile race. The same mindset shift has helped me not just physically but in other parts of my life too. When hard obstacles come at me, I deal with them completely differently because of the mindset I developed through constantly pushing myself further and further."

In 2017, Jesse invited other people to challenge their own mindsets to see what they could do if they pushed themselves as well, forming a group he called "We Do Hard Stuff." He put his money where his mouth was, too, offering to donate $100 of his own money to a charity of people's choice if they completed hard challenges every month. In just the first few months of the year, he donated more than $150,000 as a result of regular people all around the world pushing themselves like they had never pushed themselves before.

"We took people from average to savage. People who hadn't done a burpee in years did 2017 burpees in one month. Moms of four with busy schedules. Lawyers with full days. Musicians on the road. All different kinds of people from all walks of life challenged themselves to participate in fitness challenges they never dreamed possible until they committed to developing a 'savage' mindset."

Jesse's experience, and the experience of the moms, lawyers, musicians, and others, demonstrates one important principle to follow if you want to Broker Billions. It doesn't matter what your background is today, you can do much more than you might imagine when you train your brain to forget what other people might assume is possible for you. You can achieve much more than you ever imagined if you commit to developing the mindset of a billion-dollar broker and take action with that in mind. That's what Jesse did. That's what the moms, lawyers, and musicians did. That's what all the billion-dollar brokers whom I featured in this book did. And there's no reason that can't be you too.

Legends Are Made, Not Born

Building a Billion-Dollar Mindset starts with accepting the truth that there's nothing separating you, me, or any other top broker in the world except for the steps we've taken to date. We all have our strengths and weaknesses. For example, I am very self-aware, so when I started the process of becoming a top broker, I had a pretty good understanding of what parts of the business I should focus on and what parts I should delegate or outsource. Because I also have dyslexia and ADHD, it tends to make it more challenging to rise to the top of an industry without help from others. Your advantages and disadvantages will be different, but you'll learn how to focus on your advantages and get help to not let your disadvantages hold you back (we'll talk about this later in the book).

As the old saying goes, "Legends aren't born—they're made." Yet the majority of folks go to their grave selling themselves short, thinking there's some reason why they can't achieve big goals.

Some people think there's something wrong with *them* that will hold them back. In my case, that might be my dyslexia or ADHD. Other people think they can't market or network if they're introverted or can't negotiate contracts if they don't have a business mind.

Other people think there's something wrong with *their environment* that holds them back. In my case, that could have been getting my first listing in 2009 in a market with nineteen thousand other agents competing for listings. Other people think they can't succeed because they're in a rural area or a highly competitive suburban market that already has a well-regarded broker.

Or people don't believe they can make a few simple tweaks to break the mold of conventional wisdom to stand out enough to rise to the top of their market. When I got started, I didn't have access to something like the Brokering Billions system. I had to figure out how to stand out from others on my own. I now help hundreds of agents at my company, and even more outside of my company, stand out using the strategies I developed.

These beliefs are dangerous, untrue, and have caused way too many agents to work way too hard, make way too little money, and live a life far different from their dream life because it causes people to not take action.

They live a life of complacence—never exploring anything "exceptional"—stuck running in the middle of the pack. They have unique personal strengths they don't play to, life-changing habits they don't implement, and opportunities for success they don't pursue.

Well, I have good news for you. I'm about to delve into some harsh truths I've learned on this journey to the top with the goal of helping you leave this chapter knowing the truth—that the only difference between you, me, and the other top brokers I'll introduce you to in this book is the actions we have taken to date.

There's no reason why you can't achieve tremendous levels of success in *any* environment when you take the right action steps.

And, when you play to your strengths and take a simple but innovative approach to selling real estate, you truly *can* stand out from the crowd to become a top broker just like me.

Start Where You Are and Run Your Own Race

While following a proven system like this one will give you an advantage and help you move faster, an important step toward developing a Billion-Dollar Mindset is to accept that you are where you are, you can't start from anywhere but there, and you must run your own race. This is one of the toughest concepts to accept. Many highly motivated people, like me, are also tremendously impatient. We know it can take time to achieve big goals, but we want to move fast. We see others ahead of us and wish we had what they have already.

While you can give yourself an advantage by getting help from someone like me, the only place you can start is from where you are. You might look around and see a competitor with more money to throw at marketing. Or you might look at someone who has ten more years of relationships. Or you might see someone you think is smarter or more charismatic than you.

Those factors can certainly make things easier for those other brokers, but they have nothing to do with you, so you can't let that frustration hold you back. You *must* let that frustration go.

The best brokers became top brokers because they learned how to develop a Billion-Dollar Mindset, which is all about multiplying, being obsessed with envisioning what you want to do and how you want to get there. It's an obsessive, undefeated, and disruptive mindset that keeps you moving forward no matter what obstacles you face. It becomes your competitive advantage and can help you overcome any advantage your competition seemingly enjoys.

The Billion-Dollar Mindset

Human nature is not to be good. Human nature is not to be great. Human nature is to survive. That's drinking water and eating rice. It's not in our DNA to necessarily go out and do exceptional things. Too many people buy into the myth that they have genetically inherited a certain level of ambition and are stuck at that level for the rest of their lives. I'm here to tell you that notion is 100 percent false. You must be completely and utterly obsessed with where you want to go, and the rest will follow.

We should all want to thrive. When I walked into the real estate office that hired me in 2009, I was determined to be the number one agent in Atlanta during my first year. That's a pretty lofty goal. I was thirty-two years old, saying I wanted to be the number one agent. The only way for it to happen was for me to be 100 percent obsessed with making it happen. Everything I did was focused on selling real estate, networking, and letting everyone in Atlanta know that I could sell their home faster and for more money than anyone else. Period. End of story.

When you possess the Billion-Dollar Mindset, you wholeheartedly believe that nothing is out of your reach! In other words, anything you want is 100 percent possible if you're willing to rewire your brain toward success, abundance, and happiness in both your work life and your relationships.

People said, "God, there goes Bonneau again. That guy's crazy. He sure does post a lot online. Why is he always marketing? Why doesn't he just do regular-size postcards—why does he send them out three times bigger than they need to be? What's he trying to prove?" Quiet the voices; replace them with positive statements about yourself, your potential, and your future. Make these affirmations your mantras; they will energize and sustain you. Repeat them until you believe them and until they manifest in your life.

The voices inside and outside your head dramatically impact your odds for future growth and success. Whether their effect is positive or negative is determined by which ones you listen to. You have the power to filter out anything that doesn't serve your goals.

Extraordinary success requires you to do extraordinary things. You've got to think ten times bigger than everybody else. You've got to work ten times harder and market ten times more than your competitors. You've got to get up earlier and produce ten times more. This applies to every aspect of your life: it relates to spending time with your spouse, playing in the yard with your kids, and amping up your workout to stay healthy and in shape. It's an all-encompassing concept.

When Your Mindset Holds You Back

Although Holly Parker consistently sells hundreds of millions of dollars of real estate per year, there was a time when she had been stuck working and selling in the same price range for a while.

"I really had to get under my own hood because I started seeing that, as we all do, I was at that moment being my own worst enemy," Holly explains, as she describes how her mindset had become disconnected from the most important factors to keep growing.

"I realized that there was this connection to value that I had lost. I wasn't valuing myself enough. In some ways, I think there was some sort of punishment or self-sabotage going on in my head, almost as if I was telling myself, *you don't deserve to continue growing.* It wasn't until I truly started valuing myself that I was able to break through the plateau to reach new heights."

With Holly, as it does with many of us, it took her becoming deliberate with her self-praise to overcome the negative scripts she had been telling herself. "Finally, I told myself, *wait a minute, wait a minute, you do deserve this, you're awesome.* I realized that I was way too good at championing and encouraging people, and I needed to do the same for myself. I am the number one cheerleader for my clients, but I needed to be the number one cheerleader for me. I needed to be my own best advocate."

With that one shift, Holly was back on a growth track to building the business and life of her dreams.

Start with the End in Mind

As real estate agents, we all start each year at zero. There's the old pit in the stomach. How am I going to do it again? Who else feels this way on January 1? Every year, we are forced to create new baselines, so you might as well get good at it and aim high.

On January 1, I consciously set a clear sense of where I want to go. Let's say I was at $100 million and wanted to get to $150 million. On January 1, I start thinking and acting like a $150 million agent. What does that mean? Maybe I hire another assistant. Maybe I bring in additional technology to keep up with $50 million more business. I start the year top-heavy, knowing I will need the extra help as we move into the year. I always hit my goals. Why? Because I stay obsessed.

I have to have a path to reach my goals. As my friend Jesse Itzler says, "How you do anything is how you do everything." It goes back to the old saying, "Are you going to do what you want to do, or are you going to do what you need to do?" If you're not on point with everything in your life, if you're not 10x-ing everything, you're going to fail.

But that is true in any industry.

Take Kirby Smart, the head football coach at the University of Georgia. I'm a huge Georgia Bulldogs and Kirby Smart fan. The man truly has an undefeated mindset and, in 2021, coached the Bulldogs to their first national championship since 1980. In his first year coaching the team, 2016, he held the team to an 8–5 record. His second: 13–2 and an SEC conference title. His third: 11-3 and an SEC Eastern Division title. By 2021, they were national champions.

Although his football knowledge and strategies are second to none, his mindset is what has impressed me most about Kirby. For example, a few years ago, he was asked about his approach:

"I don't think you ever arrive," Kirby said. "I could be sitting here in Year 10 and there's still got to be growth. If you don't grow, then what are you doing? Why are you doing this profession? I challenge our guys to do the same thing, our staff. If you are sitting here doing the same thing you did last year, then we're not going anywhere, because other people around us, they are changing and developing and getting better, and if we're not doing that then we are going to get passed by."[1]

This is how we start each year as well. You create a baseline, and then you build on that baseline. After you hit a level, there's always another level. You have to keep rising. Set your goal and work backward, mapping out each step down to the tiniest movement—everything you need to do to reach your goal.

We were all so devastated about Kobe Bryant's passing. I had admired him for many years, and at a certain point, decided to

---

1   Mike Griffith, "Kirby Smart's Fascinating Dive into Georgia Football Philosophy," DawgNation, July 24, 2019, https://www.dawgnation.com/football/kirby-smart-georgia-uga-banquet-coach/.

study his mindset. I found out that he used to get up at 4 a.m. to train. He wasn't the tallest; he wasn't the fastest; he couldn't jump the highest—but he had a Billion-Dollar Mindset and a desire to win and spent hours in the gym mastering the techniques he needed to become one of the greatest basketball players in history.

With a Billion-Dollar Mindset, you wake up each morning and ask yourself where you want to go and what's most important for you to get there. And that allows you to focus on the most important activities and not waste time dealing with less important calls for your attention. What's important? Thinking about new strategies, your vision, and how you're going to take yourself from $20 million to $40 million, $50 million to $100 million, $150 million, and so on. Or maybe you'd even like to start your own business. But if you waste time dealing with all the seemingly "urgent" but less important calls for your attention, you'll end up just spinning the proverbial hamster wheel and keep it rolling until you burn out.

Once you have the Billion-Dollar Mindset, you've got to create a path to get where you want to go. I call this process identifying your target. I want to teach you how to focus to work smarter, not harder. We'll talk about that in the next chapter.

How You Do Anything is How You do Everything When Brokering Billions

The concept that "how you do anything is how you do everything" is not just a catchy phrase that you print on a poster and hang in your office.

For example, Jesse Itzler is a high achiever. He gets stuff done. That's part of his identity. But, one day, he was watering the garden when his wife called him in for dinner. So, he dropped the hose and started walking in, thinking to himself that he'd put the hose away the next day. The moment he caught himself thinking about leaving the hose out overnight, he stopped in his tracks. He was so disciplined in the message that "how you do anything is how you do everything" that he did not want to be the type of person who would put things off until the next day no matter how minor it might seem. So he turned around, put away the hose, and went in for dinner.

If you want to Broker Billions, it needs to be your way of life, too. You need to decide what type of agent do you want to be and then use that as a filter for everything you do, even when nobody is watching.

For example, let's assume that part of how you want to be known is as the most professional, organized, proactive, and resourceful agent in your area. How should it look like when you show up to a listing meeting?

Should you pull up ten minutes late in a beat-up car filled with burger wrappers, with one side of your shirt untucked, taking notes on a single piece of paper? Do you ask for a pen because you forgot yours? Do you shake their hand with the grip of a toddler and without making eye contact?

Of course not. You start preparing for that meeting the second you wake up in the morning. From the way you get out of bed. You don't roll out of bed and complain out loud about all the work you have to do. You get up, fix your bed nice and neat and get ready to start your day. You brush your teeth. You eat a healthy breakfast and clean up after yourself. Before you leave, you check your calendar to confirm nothing changed from the night before.

Well before the meeting, your assistant confirms any traffic or other issues that would prevent you from showing up on time and adjust as necessary. You get your professional packet together that you bring and give yourself plenty of time to arrive a few minutes early. After all, you're the professional, organized agent. You'd make sure you're on time.

Of course, your car is clean and organized. You make sure not to block in any cars in their driveway. You ring the doorbell right on time. When the door opens, your next client sees a well-dressed, agent with a professional smile. You extend you hand for a firm handshake and make eye contact. You walk in with integrity and you continue with the same professional, organized approach, showing them all the proactive and resourceful things you've done already, even before they hire you. You leave with the listing, as usual.

To Broker Billions you need to be the most consistent person on the face of the earth. From the way you dress to the way you talk to the way you stand, greet strangers, record a voicemail, talk with your family, and even address personal tasks.

Is your voicemail greeting the standard "I can't get to the phone. Please leave your name, number, and a brief message and I'll call you back when I can."

Or, is it, "You've reached Bonneau Ansley at (404) 484-4663. I'm so sorry I missed your call. Please leave me a detailed message and let me know how I can serve you and I'll call you back as soon as I can."

When you meet new people, do you give a professional smile and firm handshake.

When greet the person serving you for dinner, do you barely look up and mumble your order or do you make sure to get their name and treat them with kindness and respect?

When you get out of bed, do you leave your bed and bedroom a mess?

When someone's assistant brings you a drink during a meeting do you thank them by name?

When you leave that meeting do you leave your plate on the table or do you clean up after yourself?

Do you dress for success?

Do you treat others with kindness?

And, when nobody's watching, do you put things off or do you still get things done?

Do you focus on doing everything you do a little bit better throughout the day?

How you do anything is how you do everything.

Be consistent. Be professional. Be the Billion-Dollar Agent in everything you do.

To Shoot for the Stars, We Must Break the Mold

If it ain't broke, break it.

—Thad Wong

As children, we are often taught that disruption is a bad thing. It lands you in the principal's office or in after-school suspension. The mere act of disrupting a class, lesson, or activity is frowned upon. You don't get rewarded for this perceived negative type of behavior, and you certainly aren't going to find any substantial advantages as a kid in being disruptive.

As a fifth grader and legacy at one of the most prestigious schools in Atlanta, I found myself in the principal's office almost every day. While my sister sailed along at the top of her class, seemingly without effort, each afternoon after school I dragged my old toys to the bottom of our driveway at homework time and flagged down cars, trying to sell my so-called prized possessions. Even then I was a salesman.

As parents, we generally strive to raise children who fit in, collaborate, get along well with other children, and are comfortable with the world around them. Fitting in almost becomes the mantra for our youth, a steadfast pillar we inject into their very existence. Conventional society so often casts asides the dreamers—those who are brave, creative, and disregarding of boundaries. Because we are trained to stay inside the box, it then becomes virtually unacceptable to think outside of it. But staying inside the box is where creativity goes to die and where productivity is stifled. That, my friend, is where we fail our children. And that, despite my best intentions, is where I failed, through no fault of my own, as I struggled to find a positive and productive place for myself growing up.

These children, many just like me, grow up trying to fit in, doing everything in their power to mirror their peers. They shy away from disruption and expressing their "true selves," all because they don't receive positive reinforcement when they express themselves. They're told at a young age that thinking differently is a bad thing. With that kind of advice, the fire in the child's spirit is extinguished, the mind confined. Get the picture? The black-and-white, cookie-cutter image remains, free of any real color or character. In truth, we are ultimately doing our children and our society a grave injustice by crafting a negative connotation around disruption.

Why? Because innovation gets beat out of us at a young age. To develop a Billion-Dollar Mindset, we need to fight back against our original conditioning and be willing to stand out.

Standing Out

As our children mature into young adults, choose a career, and join the professional world, well-positioned disruption can become a game changer, a path to forging something uniquely their own, something that will make them stand out and thrive. Those few adults who retain their childhood ability to wonder and to disrupt can develop an amazing competitive advantage. They can mature to be head and shoulders above the rest. It's their tremendous grit that can, with training and mentorship, position them to become remarkable leaders and creative thinkers. They might have stopped acting out in class, but they never abandoned their desire to be different or their focus on not always conforming.

In the business world, it's the disrupters who can become the pacemakers for the race—or, better said, the marathon—of life. They often lead the pack, living at the forefront of their respective industries. In many ways, this notion of productive disruption becomes *the* competitive advantage. And it's not something that's frequently nurtured. In fact, there's too much pressure from parents on being "normal." That can kill a person's competitive advantage early in life. Our most celebrated disrupters are those who maintain their disruptive nature despite the status quo rulebook that otherwise could have stood in their way.

The "Right" Kind of Disruptive

If you've ever seen the cartoon Jimmy Neutron, Jimmy, the lead character, is a kid who has an abnormally large brain that helps him to think more "genius" thoughts than most people. Jimmy, like some folks, has an IQ that he can certainly use to his advantage. But just because he can think scientifically doesn't mean he has that "loaded" pair of dice. Challenge Jimmy to a song number or dance and I'm sure you'll have him beat. It's all about finding where your zone is—we all have an area in our lives where we're capable of a "brain blast."

While we're all equipped for survival, we're not all equipped with the same strengths and weaknesses (we'll get to this in a bit). Disruption, namely, is a natural and innate quality with which some of us are born. We might not know it at the time, but we are often the freethinkers, destined to fly.

For me, the first eighteen years of my life were a push and pull tug-of-war of trying to use my disruptive nature for good, not something to be stifled. I loved getting attention as a child, and quickly became the class clown. Thank goodness for this, because at least my classmates had their eyes on me and loved the spectacle. It prevented me from being down and dour about my academic struggles. But my teachers weren't having it and often sent me to the hallway to "reflect" on my behavior. That didn't stop me. With every laugh and pat on the back from my classmates, I only felt more empowered to continue my disruptive ways.

Only when I experienced learning outside of the classroom did I discover that I could channel my disruptive personality into something that actually benefited me. That's when I started my first business at an all-boys boarding school in Virginia—Woodberry Forest, where I attended high school. I developed an early sense of independence by going away to school when I was barely a teenager and made lifelong friends who are still like brothers to me.

In my junior year, I started selling T-shirts and hats with creative messaging to my fellow classmates. I found a local printer that could silk-screen images onto these shirts and hats. I would receive packages from them, and then shove the goods into my backpack and run around the dorms selling and selling, all the while honing my sales skills. My top T-shirt slogan was "We Don't Need Girls Here; We're Doing Fine with Yours." And my most famous and lucrative product was a baseball hat I created for one of the longest-running high school rivalries in the country, the Woodberry vs. Episcopal High School football game—always dubbed "The Game." This was The Game's one-hundredth year, and I created thousands of hats and sold them to both Woodberry and Episcopal students, faculty, and alumni, capitalizing on both schools. I thought big and I killed it.

After just a few months of selling T-shirts and hats, I had more cash than I knew what to do with. This was similar to the stockpile I developed as a child from selling my toys. The school got wind of my business and made me put my cash in the school vault. The business eventually transitioned with me to college at the University of Georgia.

During my freshman year at UGA, I decided it was time to formalize the T-shirt company beyond what I had done in high school. I knew I needed some further seed money. I was racking my brain with where to turn and thought I had seized upon a brilliant idea in approaching my father. I went to him and, with little forethought, offered to sell him my car. I hadn't considered what I would do without it. "Well, son," he said, after a long drag on his Marlboro Light, "I already own that car."

I would have to look elsewhere. I started with what I had, found a couple of partners, and grew the business from there. I called my little enterprise the Yellow 5 T-shirt Company, based on the dye used often in the silk-screening process. Soon, using my natural salesmanship, I had the University of Georgia's fraternity and sorority market cornered, selling T-shirts to them for all their weekend parties. We printed T-shirts on our used silk screen machine for almost eighteen hours per day. We kept growing until I eventually sold the business. That was when I knew I had made the hustle real.

In my junior year, I decided to take my first real estate class at the University of Georgia's Terry College of Business. From the first moment, I was hooked. I remember it vividly because it was one of the first times in my entire life that I found myself in a hyperfocused zone, truly locked in. It was also one of the first times I didn't feel like I needed to cheat the system. I wanted to do all my own work. It was at that moment in class that I quickly decided to dive headfirst into the industry, using some of my newfound knowledge and enthusiasm to get a real estate license. Twenty-five years later, I'm still as passionate as ever about the business.

It was about that time that I started receiving positive reinforcement for my disruption. It was no longer seen as a negative and punishable trait, as I was getting straight As and was engaged in my studies like never before. Looking back through my years of schooling, I think I always had a sense of productive disruption; it was just a matter of how to channel it in a positive way in a world that often has little tolerance for the unconventional. It wasn't like I strove to be the class clown as I did in elementary school; it was my way of coping and expressing myself in an environment where I didn't fit and wasn't succeeding. And I certainly didn't enjoy the endless barrage of parent-teacher meetings. Those car rides home were painful.

Have you ever felt that way? Like you couldn't fully connect and find purpose until you found something that mattered to you? That you loved? That seemed to be your passion?

Productive disruption starts with loving what you do. It is a function of true engagement, knowing that you not only can give 100 percent but also really want to.

Train Your Brain

Although each of the agents I interviewed for this book demonstrates a mindset that helped them stand out from the crowd, Josh Anderson's reaction to my question about mindset was worth sharing.

Josh served eight years in the US Army, including a ten-month stint in Bagram, Afghanistan, during Operation Enduring Freedom. As such, you'd expect him to have developed a virtually unmatched mindset.

When I asked him what characteristics agents need to have to become great, he immediately identified "grit" as the standout characteristic. Yes, you need to have the basics in place because, as he described it, "the basics work, and you can always build the foundation of basics and then get creative." But "when I'm talking to my team, I emphasize six things: mindset, database, scripts, knowing your numbers, lead generation, and time blocking. Those are the six factors we train on."

While many people expect leaders like Josh to train on scripts, numbers, lead generation, database, and even time management or time blocking, they don't often identify mindset as one of just six topics that top agents train intentionally to improve.

Similarly, agent Leigh Marcus makes mindset a daily focus. In 2021, he sold 329 units representing close to $230 million in volume. Before getting into real estate, he was in corporate technology sales. His wife was in real estate. He saw what she was doing and thought the opportunity was astronomical if he could bring the same corporate approach he took in technology sales, with sophisticated systems, processes, and accountability to the real estate world. While that's exactly what he did, I'll talk more about the systematic approach Leigh takes to selling real estate in later chapters.

With someone so systematic about systems and processes, it might surprise you to learn that he doesn't start every morning by making phone calls, catching up on paperwork, or doing research. Yes, he gets on the phone by 7:30 a.m. (one of the habits he borrowed from technology sales). But his day starts with mindset (and much earlier than 7:30 a.m.).

"I feel like how you start your day is everything. How you start your day is how your day goes. I usually start my day at about 4:15. I get up, get ready, exercise, and try to get to the office by about 5:15 or 5:30," Leigh explains. What does he do for two hours before his daily phone call habit begins? I do a lot of mindset exercises. Meditation, planning the day, gratitude, affirmation, and getting my head right before getting on the phone to start the workday."

Just like his physical exercise trains his body, Leigh's daily mindset exercises build strong mental muscles that keep him focused and productive. Mindset isn't like a light switch. You need to exercise it daily to get—and stay—at the top of your game.

The Passion Problem

Before we move forward, let me say a little bit more about the role of passion when it comes to Brokering Billions. As the old saying goes, "Follow your passion and you'll never work a day in your life."

Unfortunately, that saying will cause you to become miserable way more than it will lead you to success and happiness in real estate or any other career.

Even worse, it can cause you to hate something you were once passionate about because it raises false hope. It can even cause you to doubt your ability to succeed at anything in your life.

Passion is important. You've heard me mention it a few times already. It's definitely helpful. There's no doubt about that.

But passion is just the *fuel* that pushes you up the ladder in whatever career you choose—especially in real estate. Why? Despite what people who have never sold a house in their life might think, selling real estate isn't easy. You don't just show a property, send a few emails, and collect a commission. If that were the case, you probably wouldn't be reading this book. You'd be Brokering Billions already.

Thus, having a passion for real estate, business, selling, and people can help motivate you to keep going when times are tough. But if all you have is passion, quit now. Save yourself from the pain, frustration, and even embarrassment that comes with trying to achieve something on passion alone.

You need much more than passion to succeed in real estate.

You need to be great at what you do.

You need to be innovative—or have someone on your team be innovative if that's not your natural style.

You need to be willing to put in the hard work to become better—even when you're already great.

You need the will and determination to push forward even when everything seems to be crashing down around you.

You need to be willing to sacrifice a lot in the present to achieve even more in the future.

Yes, passion can be the fuel that keeps you going. Having a deep and important reason—a "why" as we say in business—helps you keep going when the pain of the present feels almost too big to handle.

But if you only have passion, the best thing you can do is quit because passion without talent, hard work, smart work, and sacrifice will cause you to just spin your wheels for a longer period.

So, if you want to become an agent—and not just any agent but one of the top agents—forget about "following your passion."

Instead, wake up every morning and tell yourself you're going to do what it takes to

- be great today,
- act like the top agents act,
- think like top agents think,
- work smarter than your competition so you can achieve more in less time, and
- push through the obstacles and challenges the day brings.

If you have been struggling to build your volume, you can still become a top agent. But passion won't get you there.

Instead, begin every day by telling yourself those five simple bullet points and then following through with them throughout the day. If you do that consistently for the next year, I have no doubt you can become one of the top agents in your area, reduce your working hours, and love your work (no matter what the real estate market looks like).

Turn Your "Challenges" into Your Superpowers

I'll be the first to admit, it took a miracle to keep my attention, except when the subject matter interested me. You could say my greatest limitation early on was my inability to focus on peripheral matters, engage for longer periods with them, and concentrate on matters that seemed unrelated to my life. In many ways, I think this trained me early on to see the bigger picture and focus on the larger trends. This, along with my determination and faith that I would ultimately be okay, would later be a huge asset for me in business. In general, I was a happy person and didn't feel disadvantaged or flawed. And I knew I could outwork anybody.

It's not that I didn't want to succeed in school. Rather, I couldn't. I literally was not wired with the ability to focus on the singular tasks or responsibilities that were presented to me in the classroom. I disrupted class as a way to cope with these limitations. I didn't set out to be a troublemaker, but the attention I got from my disruption spurred me on and balanced out the discouragement I heard coming from teachers each day, not to mention the threats from the principal that I might have to go to another school. Frankly, I didn't care.

In my case, out of a class of twenty-five people, five of us were sent to the corner of the room with a special teacher whose job was to try to bring us up to speed. I was constantly placed in that corner of the room, along with the same four other classmates. And we had the best time. I realized then that none of the teachers really got me. And I didn't get them either. I wanted to get out of there.

Everybody has their own set of limitations; I don't care who you are. As a child, your shortcomings can make you feel inferior, but in my case, strangely enough, they didn't. I turned my limitations into a game, a game so intricate and fascinating it never ceased to engage me. Strategizing my next move fueled me and ultimately became one of my superpowers. I continued to up the ante and pull bigger and funnier stunts. When you're a kid, other children might tease you or make fun of you because you have a specific weakness or imperfection, but again, it didn't happen for me in that way. My classmates didn't tease me because I was so funny. My popularity grew because of the stunts I pulled.

It didn't take a professional to tell me I had issues with my brain's ability to comprehend and digest what I considered trivial information. I knew I couldn't spell, and that I struggled with pronunciation. I would look at a page, and the words could appear reversed, out of place, and extremely hard to understand, which did put me at an extraordinary disadvantage in a traditional school setting. The simple task of reading was an uphill battle, but I didn't let it discourage me. This also helped me learn not to take orders. I was not about to become an order-taker, from teachers or anyone else. I have never worked for anyone other than myself and probably wouldn't have lasted in a corporate setting.

As I looked around my classroom, I often noticed other kids engaged, turning pages in their books, and clearly understanding the words in front of them. I, on the other hand, couldn't wait until any reading exercise came to an end. It was painful at best, and a horrible obstacle at worst. Comprehending simple words on a page felt like pushing a thousand-pound boulder uphill. I knew I was falling behind. It should probably have created anxiety for me, but I had faith that one day I would be released from that prison and be free to channel my wit and passion into something remarkable.

But like anything, humans evolve and adapt. And that's exactly what I did. From a young age, I quickly realized the only way I would overcome my limitations was through wit and persistence. I had to work twice as hard as other kids just to keep up. I developed reading and learning hacks—tips and tricks that helped me fill in the blanks and keep up. I might have been behind in one type of comprehension, but I was developing a strong ability to think outside the box and innovate to get the job done. Eventually, I realized my refusal to focus on stuff that doesn't matter, the core of my ADHD, offered me a remarkable opportunity to multitask. Because I was capable of simultaneously juggling multiple balls in the air and jumping from one job to the next, I could easily take on much more than most. My ADHD created a sense of obsession within—if I felt the job was worth it. If I was interested in a topic or an activity, I could laser focus until I got the job done. I didn't waiver; I didn't stray. Sheer, intense focus.

While my ADHD and eventually my diagnosis of dyslexia both started as limitations, I quickly turned them into two of my greatest assets. Now, as an adult, I wonder where I would be without these so-called limitations. I built Ansley through determination and focus. As I'm writing this book, I'm also leading my team of four hundred-plus agents, selling more houses than anyone else in the South, and vetting investment opportunities. Most importantly, I'm always striving to be the best husband and father I can be. Funnily enough, my inability to focus on only one thing at a time is now the path to my diversification and success. God gave me some bitter lemons, and I found a way to make some pretty tasty lemonade.

Your Mindset as Power to Thrive during Slow Markets

When I started writing this book, the market was still hot. Interest rates were low. People were upgrading, downsizing, buying second homes, and moving all over the country. As I finish this book, there's no doubt the market is slowing down, for many reasons. That's natural and can even be good news for the best agents around, as it'll likely cause many agents to leave the industry.

So how do you survive, or even thrive, in down markets? If you ask Mark Spain, it starts with mindset.

"It's just mindset," Mark told me, emphasizing that agents were spoiled in 2021 and the first half of 2022 when people spent on homes in a way that's not normal. "You have to understand that 3 percent interest rates are not normal." However, Mark also noted that 5 percent or 5½ percent interest is still cheap money, and that people are still moving from other places, even if they aren't moving around within cities as much.

"Are there going to be as many deals going around? No. But you better roll up your sleeves and become the best you can be because we're getting ready. We've already rolled our shirt sleeves up. We're getting after it, and we're going to take our 'unfair share' because that's what you do in these kinds of markets. You can't just put your head in the sand. You can't just sit and complain about everything. You have to get at it because many people need a place to live, and it's our job to provide that service. Get up every day at the same time, work out, eat healthy, do the things you need to do."

Your Mindset as Fuel to Get Through Anything That Comes Your Way

In 2010, Johnny Ussery was driving home from Atlanta after watching his son play baseball for Georgia Tech, where he attended on a baseball scholarship. Johnny wasn't feeling right, so he decided to schedule a doctor's appointment that Monday afternoon.

The appointment went well, with the doctor describing Johnny as "healthy as a horse." But he decided to get some blood work and a urine sample just to see what was going on.

The following day, the doctor called Johnny, and this time he was not as upbeat. He told Johnny to avoid eating anything and to get to the hospital for a scan at 2:00 that afternoon. He said he found something in the blood work he didn't like. And he also told Johnny he was going to come by his house at 5:00 that evening.

"It's not usually a good sign when your doctor is coming to your house," Johnny recalls, also noting that he and his doctor were long-time personal friends. "When he came to my house, he sat down and started crying before breaking the silence to tell me, 'John, you have pancreatic cancer, and there's an 85 percent chance you won't live past five months.'" He further explained that only 15 percent of people qualify for surgery, but surgery could increase his odds significantly.

"By God's grace and great medical care, I did fall in that 15 percent who had a chance," Johnny explains. "They did what they call a 'Whipple procedure' where they took out parts of my stomach, appendix, duodenum, and my gallbladder and then try to hook everything back up. Then they gave me six months of chemo followed by radiation and more chemo. They threw the kitchen sink at me. But by God's grace and great medical care, I'm here talking with you twelve years later. Only 5 percent survive five years. So you won't hear me complaining about being too hot today or too cold. I'm just happy to be here."

Johnny likes to tell a short story about two twin boys, whom he calls Billy and Bobby, to demonstrate how having a positive mindset and attitude can impact you. Billy was an eternal optimist. Bobby was an eternal pessimist.

Concerned about their boys, the parents decided to take the kids to a child psychologist. The psychologist decided to put the optimist in a room full of horse manure and the pessimist in a room full of toys to see how they reacted.

A short while later, the psychologist and the parents returned. When they entered the room with the toys and the pessimist, they were surprised to see the boy sitting in the corner sucking his thumb. When they asked why he hadn't ridden the bike, the boy said he was afraid he would fall off and skin his knee. When they asked why he didn't play computer games, the boy said he didn't like computer games. All the boy saw in that room was negativity.

When they entered the room with the manure and the optimist, it was a completely different story. The boy was in the middle of the manure throwing it all over the place. It was on the walls, getting in the hall, and even splattering all over the parents and the doctor. When they asked the boy what he was doing, the boy responded, "With all this horse manure in here, there has to be a pony somewhere."

Fortunately, many agents won't be facing a 15 percent likelihood of dying in five months or a room full of manure anytime soon. But we will all face challenges, today, tomorrow, and in the future. We will get down. We will struggle. We will face challenges out of our control.

During those times, our attitudes can lead us in several directions. We can roll up our sleeves and fight like Johnny with his cancer diagnosis. We can look for the positives, like Billy the optimist looking for the pony among the manure. Or we can cower in the corner and suck our thumbs while our competitors take all the listings.

Let the Haters Hate

"Some people can brighten up a room just by leaving it."
—Johnny Ussery

Once you start making significant changes in your business and life, people are going to say hateful things and talk behind your back. It happened when I got started and continues to this day. It won't stop. They talk about my obsession with wanting to be the best, with doubling my business year after year, with not settling, with not slowing down. It never ends.

At first, it can be hard to hear such negativity and even jealousy about you, especially when it's based on assumptions you know to be untrue. People assumed I must be taking advantage of other people to get to the top. They assumed I must be lying or cheating to become the top agent in Atlanta my first year. They assumed I was self-centered for wanting to be the best.

And, as we'll talk about later in the book, none of it is true. In fact, the opposite is true. It *had* to be true for me to make it to the top and sustain that success. In fact, as one of my first real estate mentors Rob Thomson would tell you, "The one characteristic you need to be successful in real estate is a combination of honesty and drive. There's no such thing as a little pregnant or a little dishonest. You're either dishonest or you're not. And if you're dishonest, your days are over before you start."

If you want to become the best, you need to do it with honesty, integrity, and drive. Otherwise, it's only a matter of time before you crash and burn because your reputation is your number one asset when it comes to Brokering Billions. All the team members, systems, and marketing can't save you if nobody wants to be associated with you.

That said, no matter how strongly you *know* the hate is wrong, it doesn't make it easy to ignore. Through the years, as I have doubled and tripled my business, I've become used to it. I've become somewhat numb to it. It's become background noise. Because I know if I let it get to me, it would stand in the way of my rising to the top and helping a whole lot of people find homes, sell homes, and make a living working with me.

It took a lot of practice to be able to quiet those hateful voices, though. At first, when I heard the hate, I'd immediately repeat the opposite to myself knowing those comments said more about *them* than they said about me. When someone said, "Bonneau must be lying to people to get so many listings," I told myself they were *really* thinking *I would need to lie to people to get so many listings.* When they said, "Why doesn't he just do regular-size postcards," I told myself they were *really* thinking, *Why didn't I think to send out postcards that stood out so much?*

Over time, replacing the negativity with the truth and positive statements about myself, my potential, and my future became my affirmations, my mantras; they energized and sustained me. I repeated them until I believed them and until they manifested in my life.

The same can be true for you when you remember that the haters have no idea what's going on in your head and your heart. They don't know your "why." They don't know how well you treat people. They don't know how hard you work. So push back against their opinions by immediately replacing them with the truth.

The voices inside and outside your head dramatically impact your odds for future growth and success. Whether their effect is positive or negative is determined by which ones you listen to (yours or theirs). You have the power to filter out anything that doesn't serve your goals and replace it with the truth.

And don't even bother trying to convince them they're wrong. It doesn't work. It just robs you of time and energy that you can better direct toward your dream business or living your dream life. Let your growing reputation and extraordinary results do the talking to the haters. When you do, eventually, the people who are calling you crazy today will ask you how you did it.

The Shelf Life of a Billion-Dollar Mindset

Although a lot of people talk about developing a strong mindset when pursuing a big goal, few people talk about the *shelf life* of a Billion-Dollar Mindset. Shelf life? Yes, shelf life. That's not a typo.

So what do I mean by shelf life? I mean that a Billion-Dollar Mindset isn't a set-it-and-forget-it event. It's not a passive exercise. You don't get into the right mindset one day and move forward never again having to worry about your mindset. Far from it.

You need to reset your mindset regularly—on an annual, quarterly, monthly, weekly, daily, and sometimes even hourly or minute-by-minute basis. What does this look like?

On an annual basis, remember that, as of January 1, you have sold $0.

On a quarterly basis, track how your production compares to the same quarter last year and whether you're on track to hit your annual goals. Look for patterns or lessons to make the next quarter even more productive.

On a monthly basis, compare monthly production to the month before, the same month the previous year, and whether you're on track to hit your quarterly and annual goals. Again, look for patterns or lessons to make the next month even more productive.

On a weekly basis, make sure you didn't skip your weekly tasks, meetings, and marketing that filled your pipeline and got your team functioning at full capacity the week before.

On a daily basis, wake up with gratitude and the drive to make that day the most productive possible. Make sure you complete the daily tasks that keep your pipeline full, reputation strong, and key relationships growing.

On an hourly or minute-by-minute basis, be quick to shift into a productive and positive mindset when things go wrong—because they will. But a Billion-Dollar Mindset is resilient and quick to shift from crisis to recovery no matter what happens throughout the day.

Remember, something will go wrong every day. You will have bad days, weeks, and months. Your mindset will be tested. You might want to give up. It's in these moments when you need to get intentional about maintaining a Billion-Dollar Mindset.

When you hit reset and get right back into your Billion-Dollar Mindset when things go wrong, you can avoid making bad or desperate decisions and ensure those bad days, weeks, or even months don't keep you from rising and staying at the top of your market year after year.

Chapter 3:

Identifying Your Targets and Focus to Work Smarter Not Harder

"A goal properly set is halfway reached."

—Zig Ziglar

You've cast your vision and know exactly where you want to go and why that's so important to you. You've developed a Billion-Dollar Mindset and are ready to push forward, let the haters hate, and shift right back into your positive mindset when things go wrong.

Those are two big steps toward building the foundation of a top agent. Way too many agents skip those steps—even the ones who are committed to working hard and rising to the top. They skip over the vision and mindset work and just get right into "doing."

Although that's a natural instinct, it's dangerous. Imagine getting in your car and driving for an hour without knowing where you wanted to end up. Instead of typing a destination into your phone or GPS and letting it tell you the best route to take, you just drive until you hit an intersection and turn whichever direction looks best at the time. What are the odds you'd end up in the same place as you would if you typed in the destination and calculated the best route? Zero.

But you don't have to worry about that. You've set your destination—your vision—already by writing the final scene of your movie. And you're committed to achieving it. Now you just need the turn-by-turn directions to get there. That's what we'll talk about over the rest of the book.

In this chapter, I'm going to walk you through my process for identifying the targets and focus so you can know exactly what needs to be done—and from whom you need help—to set you up for success. (Don't worry, over the next chapters I'll show you how to find the right people to help if you don't currently have all the people you need on your team or in your network.)

Using the Multiplier Effect to Work Smarter, Not Harder

In her best-selling book, *Multipliers: How the Best Leaders Make Everyone Smarter* (HarperCollins, 2010; revised and updated, 2017), researcher, author, and executive coach, Liz Wiseman, discussed two types of leaders—Diminishers and Multipliers—and the impact of those leadership styles on the leaders, their team members, and their organizations.

Diminishers, Wiseman says, are "leaders who drain intelligence, energy, and capability from the people around them." Multipliers, on the other hand, are "leaders who use their intelligence to amplify the smarts and capabilities of the people around them." According to Wiseman, "[t]he world needs more Multipliers, especially now, when leaders are expected to do more with less."

If you want to set targets and your focus to work smarter not harder in growing your business, you can't just set a sales number that you want to hit and think you'll magically hit that goal. While setting a target sales number is a good first step, you need to then work backward from your goal to identify what each person inside and outside of your organization needs to focus on for you to hit that goal.

In other words, setting a big goal is just the first step in Brokering Billions. After setting your big goal, you need to then reverse engineer the steps it will take to achieve that goal. Next, you need to identify the steps that you're best positioned to take and the ones you'll need help with. Finally, you need to assign the steps you need help with to people inside and outside of your team to make sure everything you need to happen to achieve your goal is performed by the person or people best suited to helping you achieve it.

Then, and only then, will you have a realistic shot of achieving your big goal without having to work around the clock. After all, I didn't complete 497 transactions and sell more than $900 million in in 2021 and 2022 (while still making it home in time for dinner) by outworking other brokers in my area. In fact, when I talk to agents and other brokers in my area, one of the most common complaints I hear from them is that they work way too hard for the money they make. Some of them suggest my volume is a matter of luck. Others suggest it's a matter of having some hidden unfair advantage or trickery to get so many listings.

The truth is that there's certainly some level of my success that comes from luck. I was lucky to be born into the Ansley family. My family has great name recognition in the town where I work. I was also fortunate to go to some great schools and be able to take risks without having to worry about how I would pay for schooling, food, and other necessities.

Having said that, all those things only take you so far, and I certainly could have stopped innovating once I was making enough money to live a nice life. I could have easily stopped when I was selling $25 million, $50 million, or even $100 million. And, the truth is, if growing past those benchmarks required me to work harder and harder and harder, I would have stopped a long time ago.

But, fortunately for both you and me, Brokering Billions doesn't require you to work harder than the average agent. In fact, with the right pieces in place, you can achieve exponential growth while working substantially less than the average agent by working smarter, not harder.

So what does that look like? In many ways, all it requires is just one simple mindset shift. Once you identify the tasks that need to be done, you need to be maniacal in finding creative ways to take every possible task off your plate. The end goal is that each task will be performed in the most efficient and effective way possible, including making it so you're only doing the tasks you're great at doing (and that you actually want to do).

Smarter Lead Generation and Relationship Nurturing

So what might working smarter look like with generating leads?

In chapter 5, I'll share how building out your team frees you up to do more lead gen and who you can hire to help generate even more leads even with all that extra time freed up. In chapter 6, I'll share how to get people all over town to send you leads. In chapter 7, I'll share how to build a reputation that gets people to think of you first when looking to buy or sell. And in chapter 8, I'll share innovative marketing strategies to reach enough people to keep your pipeline full without your having to spend hours and hours pounding the pavement.

Together, these pieces of the puzzle can easily get you more leads in less time and, in many cases, help you double or even triple your production this year, provided you have the other pieces I talk about in place to handle that type of volume.

But people and processes are only two of the three ways you can work smarter, not harder to scale big. Take Rob Thomson, for example. Not only is Rob one of the most effective team leaders and marketers in the real estate space but he's also at the forefront of using real estate technology to make sure he captures as many leads from his website as possible and can contact them within minutes of them visiting his website.

How well has that worked? A few years ago, Rob got notified that someone named "Tony Robbins" had visited his site and entered his contact information to look at some properties. Although the odds of this being the actual Tony Robbins or someone entering random information were likely equal, Rob picked up the phone and dialed the number listed on the account. As soon as the person answered the phone, Rob knew. This was *the* Tony Robbins. He had logged onto the website while on his flight, and Rob called him back as he was landing. He could even hear screeching in the background as the tires hit the tarmac. Tony was impressed with Rob's responsiveness and asked to meet him the following morning to look at houses. The same technology helped Rob sell a $37 million home to the CEO of Fox News.

But the benefits of this technology don't stop at being able to call new registrants while you and their real estate search are fresh in their minds. Over time, more than 145,000 people have registered on Rob's website. Each of those people is listed in his customer relationship management software, or CRM. Every time they log into the website to view properties, their user log is updated with their name and location. And when someone in his system flies into Florida, where he works, and is logged into the system, he gets a notification and emails the agent responsible for the relationship and has them touch base with the client.

With just one simple piece of software, Rob no longer has to worry about losing a serious buyer without capturing their contact information. After all, if they are willing to enter their contact information, he knows they're serious. And he gets notifications when any lead visits Florida while looking at listings on his website. This takes all the guesswork away regarding what leads to get in touch with from his website. Again, smarter. Not harder.

Identifying Your Targets

With your final scene already written, it's time to set your sights on the targets that will help you achieve that life. This means setting long-term and short-term goals that indicate you're heading in the right direction.

For example, let's say you want to sell $100 million in homes next year. How many houses will you need to sell? It took Julie Faupel 60 homes to hit $327 million in sales in 2021 in the white-hot, high-end Jackson Hole, Wyoming, market. It took Rob Thomson a little less than 100 transactions to hit $445 million in 2021 in Florida. It took me 497 transactions to sell more than $900 million in 2021 and 2022.

Assume for our purposes that the average house you sell lists for $1 million and that prices range from $500,000 to about $3 million. Thus, to hit $100 million, you'll likely need about one hundred listings to get there.

Next, ask yourself how many listings you have currently and how many you had last year. Anywhere near one hundred? If not, you need to do something different. Maybe you need to change the makeup of your team to focus on doing the activities that get more listings while other people handle the tasks that don't need to be done by you. We'll talk about how to do that in chapter 5. Or maybe you need to build more connections around town to build brand ambassadors and have your name be thought of first when anyone mentions buying or selling a home. We'll talk about how to do that in chapter 6.

After you identify what you need to do to hit your big-picture goal, the question becomes what actions you need to take to get there. Each morning, when you wake up, ask yourself: where do I want to go? Are you going to do what you feel like doing, or are you going to do what you need to do to fulfill your goals?

With a Billion-Dollar Mindset and targets in place, you will wake up every morning focused on doing what you need to do to achieve your goals. That means, if you're at $20 million and you want to be at $50 million, you know you need to get more listings and what actions you need to take to attract more listings.

Double Your Way to Brokering Billions

From the beginning of your career, you must recognize the extraordinary value in not just setting goals that seem "reachable" when you set them, but *really big* goals—that seem completely unreachable when you set them.

Yes, I know that goes against conventional wisdom. But, again, if you want a conventional business, I'm not the guy to help you. You can't aim low if you want to Broker Billions.

Instead, you need to think bigger than your competition. Much bigger. At least double what the average agent sells in a year in your area or at least double what you did last year.

So, if you sold $1 million this year and the typical agent sells $2 million in your area, aim for at least $4 million next year. If you sold $10 million and the typical agent sells $5 million, aim for at least $20 million next year.

Yes, that might require a *big* jump for you. But that's the point. I don't want you to increase incrementally. I want you to double your way to Brokering Billions.

If they're reaching for a million dollars in sales, you can set your ceiling at five million. I call this concept "outsetting from the onset." This is based on the notion that the top goal you set will always act as your base-case scenario. You aren't going to shoot for a million dollars in sales and suddenly double that goal. Why? Because the steps you take to reach a million dollars are not going to be the same steps you'd take to do more. As legendary motivational coach and salesman Zig Ziglar said, "A goal properly set is halfway reached." So if we're going to generate big business, we've got to set big goals.

If you're going to generate more than everyone else around you, you have to think differently from everyone around you. That starts with getting serious about your goals. I start my day the night before. Before I go to bed, I start working on my action list for the next day. I write my list in a big, red hardback calendar book, the same red book I have used since 1999. I have almost twenty-five years of them stacked in my office. As the kids are getting ready for school, I add to and tweak my list, depending on what emails have come through overnight. I then launch into my day, aiming to do nothing less than outwork everyone else around me and outsell everyone in the market by a big margin. In fact, you should aim to set the trend in the industry that everyone else looks to for advice and guidance. And don't be afraid to ask for more business.

Break Down Your Big Goal into Annual Goals

Think back to the final scene you wrote earlier in the book in the context of your vision for the life you want to live. If you doubled your business every year, how long would it take for you to achieve that goal?

Even with a goal of 10x-ing your annual sales, you would need less than four years to achieve your goal if you doubled your sales every year. For example, if you want to go from $5 million to $50 million, you would hit $10 million in Year 1, $20 million in Year 2, $40 million in Year 3, and $80 million in Year 4.

So I'd encourage you to aim for doubling your sales next year, no matter what the market looks like. And, if that feels crazy, just remember that doubling your sales doesn't mean that twice as many people need to be buying or selling houses in your area next year for you to achieve your goals. All it means is that *you* need to sell twice as much next year as *you* did this year.

A *New York Times* report indicated that the number of real estate agents increased by as much as 9.6 percent (in my home market of Georgia) between January 2021 and January 2022, according to the National Association of REALTORS®, as the COVID-19 pandemic shifted the way people work and created a lot of demand for new homes.[2] Unfortunately for many of those new agents, "[a]s few as 10 percent of them will last long enough to make a full-time living selling homes."

Their loss is your gain.

You need to be ready to scoop up those listings when they (and other agents) leave the market. And with everything you're going to learn here, you'll be well positioned to do just that.

Delegate, Automate, or Eliminate Activities You Don't Need to Be Doing

Whether you're getting ready to scoop up listings as agents leave in a slowing market or dominate your area in a hot market, you *have to* get tasks off your to-do list that you have no business doing if you want to double your sales this year (and next year . . . and the year after . . . and the one after that . . .).

To start, ask yourself, what does an agent selling twice as much as I do, do all day? What do they never do? What do they have help with? What do they have multiple people doing?

For example, if you want to sell $50 million a year, there's no way you would spend all day just returning emails and texts, staying in an "urgent-cycle" world where your time and attention are directed to whatever pops up in real time.

There's no growth in that. There's no efficiency in that. There's no intentionality in that. Of course, responding to important emails is

---

2   Candace Jackson, "Why so Many People Became Real Estate Agents in the Pandemic," *New York Times*, March 4, 2022, https://www.nytimes.com/2022/03/04/realestate/real-estate-agents-pandemic.html.

critical. But important emails are the ones that *you* need to respond to right away. They are answering questions only *you* can answer. So, if you are getting stuck working on all the busy parts of your day, the important tasks that will help you double will be delayed, not done at all, or done by people who won't be as good at doing them as you. In chapter 5, I'll talk about how to build the team around you to take over the tasks you shouldn't be doing that can't be automated. For now, I just want you to start tracking what you do all day. Grab a notepad and track your activities for the next week. As you do, ask yourself whether those tacks are tasks that need to be done by *you*. (Hint: There should not be many tasks that need to be done by you.)

If something doesn't need to be done by you, put an asterisk next to it. Then, ask yourself whether that task should be delegated, automated, or eliminated. If it's something that needs to be done by a human, put a "D" next to the asterisk. Be as specific as you can too. For example, you will personally need to reply to a small number of emails. But there's no reason for you to be reading every email you receive, and you have no business responding to every email that needs a reply. A high-quality assistant should screen your emails, reply to emails that don't need your attention, flag emails that do need your attention, and get in touch with you right away when you need to see an email right away. That way, you can go in once or twice a day for fifteen minutes and reply to every email that needs your attention instead of getting notified all day by emails that distract you from doing the more important tasks. Don't worry about exactly how you're going to delegate yet. We'll talk about building your team in chapter 5.

Similarly, if a task can be automated using software, put an "A" next to it on your list and then ask your assistant to research software solutions or visit BrokeringBillions.com to find some of my favorite software solutions.

Finally, if a task doesn't need to be done at all, put an "E" next to it. Nobody should be performing that task anymore. Use that time and attention to do more productive work.

There should be very little left on your list that needs to be done by you. What should you be looking for? Think CEO activities. Seriously. Would Jeff Bezos perform those tasks at Amazon? Would Abigail Johnson perform them at Fidelity Investments? If not, the task should be on your short list to delegate, automate, or eliminate. And, although I know it might seem strange to compare yourself to Jeff Bezos's or Abigail Johnson's roles at their companies, you need to get yourself out of the mindset of doing everything yourself if you want to Broker Billions.

The only tasks that should be left for you to do are the very important tasks, such as strategizing, refining your vision, identifying how you're going to double your volume and then double it again, and *some* of the relationship building it takes to build a dedicated and high-functioning team, round out your cast, develop a billion-dollar reputation, and get more listings, although the relationship-building activities should always be shared by your team members. Yes, you need to consistently build relationships. But your team members and others should also be building relationships to help you grow.

Doubling your business doesn't happen consistently by accident. You might get lucky once or twice, especially if you're doubling from a smaller number. But to double your business and double it again and again, it takes careful planning and execution.

Delegate or Die

Jonathan Spears took a completely different approach to real estate than I did. Unlike me, who barely made it through school, Jonathan was a bit of an overachiever, to say the least.

He was homeschooled, started college at just fourteen years of age, got his first college degree at age sixteen, got his real estate license at eighteen, and earned a degree in business administration in 2011 at nineteen years old.

During one of his last semesters, Jonathan attended a recruiting event at his school. During the event, he remembers the recruiters talking about starting salaries between $30,000 and $40,000. As an entrepreneurial overachiever with his real estate license in hand, those numbers didn't impress Jonathan much, so he decided he would take a different approach and pursue a career using his real estate license.

When he decided to enter the Florida Central Coast real estate world in 2011, business was tough. The financial markets had just crashed, and a large nearby oil spill had decimated the local economy. And being so young and inexperienced, it took a while for Jonathan to find his way:

> Coming into real estate at such an early age, I didn't hit the ground running when it came to sales. I spent three or four years working as an assistant, which was pretty impactful, mainly because of the way the economy was at the time and the lack of actual transactions that were happening in the market.

> But there was a time period of incubation and growth during which I knew I was ready to go out on my own. During that time, I transitioned from more of the assistant role to showings and then to consummating the deals.
>
> Once I got my first deal under my belt, I was hooked. I couldn't just stop with one. I had to figure out how many sales I could make. From that point forward, I became focused on growth.

Although those years of training and overachievement helped prepare Jonathan for building his own book of business, he soon found out that Brokering Billions simply isn't possible if you try to do everything yourself—even for an overachiever like Jonathan.

"I quickly learned that you can't achieve exponential growth unless you delegate," Jonathan concedes. "It really boils down to delegation for me. From a growth trajectory, being able to delegate tasks has been huge. We don't have one hundred hours in the day. We have twenty-four. And how we spend the hours we're actually working are so impactful and important. And a big part of that is delegating tasks."

Outsmarting *All* Your Competition

Steve Jobs didn't set a goal to become a simple computer maker. According to Walter Isaacson, who authored Steve's biography, Jobs wanted to "infuse Apple employees with an abiding passion to create groundbreaking products and a belief that they could accomplish what seemed impossible." Now that's a pretty intensive goal—to accomplish the impossible. I seriously doubt that most other computer makers around the world were sharing a similar sentiment.

Similarly, Howard Shultz, CEO of Starbucks, made it clear from the outset he wanted to take a different approach to business. As he put it, "Risk more than others think is safe. Dream more than others think is practical." For many, a cup of coffee is a cup of coffee. From the outset, Shultz wanted to offer something so much greater than just a zap of caffeine. He says, "I saw something. Not only the romance of coffee, but . . . a sense of community. And the connection that people had to coffee—the place and one another." That is why Shultz refers to Starbucks as a "third place." The third place is a sociology-inspired concept, referring to another place outside the home and work where people can gather and build a sense of community. Schultz used the concept as a foundation in the creation of Starbucks's image as a coffee chain where people are willing to pay a bit more for coffee because of the cachet and potential connection that comes with the purchase. He's done so to the tune of more than $90 billion as of this writing.

My point in sharing these two examples is to demonstrate that it's not a mystery as to how you generate more business than others. For starters, you outdream them. You decide, early on, that you are going to set your goals much higher and make them more advanced than theirs. If your competition is selling houses, you need to sell a lifestyle. If they decide to sell a lifestyle, then you need to sell a way of life. You don't define yourself by what the other firms are offering; you offer your clients more and better. And you consider *yourself* your fiercest competitor. The second you raise the bar, you challenge yourself to raise it again. And again. And again.

Of course, when you aim high, your odds of making mistakes or not hitting your goals increase. But as Michelangelo said, "The greater danger for most of us lies not in setting our aim too high and falling short; but in setting our aim too low, and achieving our mark." He should know, as he is often celebrated as one of the most amazing goal setters in the history of our time. Throughout his entire career, Michelangelo worked in an almost obsessed fashion to outpace other artists. He constantly pushed the envelope, obsessively subscribing to the philosophy of working both smarter and harder. And, in what we could only consider to be the greatest home improvement project of his generation, if not all time, he turned the ceiling of the Sistine Chapel into one of the greatest accomplishments in the history of art. My point in sharing this lesson in art history is to show you just how important it is to set tremendous goals to generate tremendous business. You can't play small ball, ever. Aim big. Then work both hard and smart to make it happen.

Mindset Check: Thriving in Good Times and Bad

After the crash in 2008, I was able to transform my career in the face of several huge life obstacles. It wasn't easy, but I did it and you can too. In good markets and bad, in tough personal times and when you're personally thriving, with the right systems, software, and people in place, you can grow.

When I was going through tough times, I woke up each morning and made a conscious decision to lean into the future and be hopeful. I coached myself to trust my vision and my drive. I decided to expect nothing less than the best, and I knew I could build my new reality. I could see where I wanted to go—and I let nothing stop me. Now, I expect success in anything I do and commit to doing what it takes to achieve it—all while working smarter and not harder. With that mindset, opportunities are drawn to me like a magnet.

The most amazing and impactful inventions in the history of the world were created by people who had unshakable belief. Imagine how far behind we would be as a society if it weren't for these brave and visionary individuals. My own experience with adversity has taught me that real success is born out of struggle. It takes perseverance to build anything worth having. Most people mistakenly think obstacles are a drag on momentum. But the truth is that adversity forces you to develop successful habits. Every obstacle gives you the strength to face your next challenge. And that, practiced daily, is the real secret to doubling your business!

Push through Dips and Pivot from Dead Ends

Finally, when identifying targets and working through delegating, automating, and eliminating your way to working smarter, not harder, expect things to go wrong. You'll make bad decisions. Software will break. Team members will drop the ball from time to time. This is a natural part of doing the hard work it takes to make your life easier while Brokering Billions. When problems occur, you need to keep moving forward. Otherwise, you're guaranteeing your failure.

In fact, if you take the most successful people in the world, they all have only two things in common: they all started and they all kept going. They made their money in many different ways. They all have different personalities and management styles. Everyone hits obstacles. Not everyone keeps going. Be like the successful people and keep pushing forward.

Seth Godin is an author, an entrepreneur, and most of all, a teacher. By focusing on everything from effective marketing and leadership to the spread of ideas and changing literally everything, Seth has been able to motivate and inspire countless people around the world. In 2013, Seth was one of just three professionals inducted into the Direct Marketing Hall of Fame. In May 2018, he was inducted into the Marketing Hall of Fame. He might be the only person in both. Back in 2007, Seth authored *The Dip: A little Book That Teaches You When to Quit (and When to Stick)* (Piatkus). In that book, he describes the concept of the Dip. He shares with his readers that winners are really the best quitters. He shows us that "winners quit fast, quit often, and quit without guilt—until they commit to beating the *right* Dip." That is where significance occurs—when you commit to beating the right Dip.

Everyone hits a Dip. I did. You likely already have. And when you want to Broker Billions, you will hit another Dip at some point too. For example, during the same year I started Ansley | Christie's International Real Estate, I thought it would be a great idea to start a construction company as well, knowing that many of my clients would have construction needs.

A few months in, I realized I had taken on the wrong partner to manage the construction segment of my firm. I had little control over him and the fifty to sixty subcontractors it takes to build a house, not to mention the unpredictability of the timing and costs of construction projects.

My name was on dozens of new construction projects, and I didn't like how things were going, which put me in a vulnerable position. I quickly decided that this part of my business would hurt my reputation and take my eyes off building a big brokerage. I decided I should fold the construction business and chalk it up to the cost of learning a quick, early lesson. The squeeze wasn't worth the juice with that business. To this day, I'm still convinced it saved me lots of future pain.

I hit another challenge a couple of years later, although in this case, I discovered that the challenge wasn't really a "Dip" that needed me to keep pushing but more of a total dead end that needed a pivot. I had heard great things about a successful agent team from another brokerage firm. I reached out to them and asked whether they wanted to jump onboard at Ansley. Within a week, many of our staff members, who would never intentionally rock the boat, had come to me to say the new agents were rude, pushy, and didn't gel with our DNA. I knew right away it wasn't the right fit. At the end of the day, I made a tough decision to send them on their way within a week of hiring them. It was awful for me *and* them. But, in the end, it made us a much stronger company.

Every new project (or job, or hobby, or company) starts out fun, then gets really hard and not much fun at all. You might be in a Dip—a temporary setback that will get better if you keep pushing. But maybe it's a total dead end. What sets superstars apart is the ability to tell the two apart. Winners seek out Dips. They realize that the bigger the barrier, the bigger the reward for getting past it. If you can beat the Dip to be the best, you'll earn profits, glory, and long-term security. You'll find significance. Whether you're an intern or a CEO and times are tough, it is crucial to determine whether you're facing a Dip that's worthy of your time, effort, and talents.

If it is, you should double down on your efforts to think big, set goals, and work smarter. If not, it might be time to cut bait, redirect your efforts and attention to something more profitable, and chalk up the time and money you already spent as tuition for the lessons learned in the process.

Chapter 4:

Cultivating the Billion-Dollar Habits and Hobbies to Help You Consistently Grow

In chapter 2, I talked briefly about the impact that Kobe Bryant's mindset had on his career. With only a high school education, Kobe not only built an all-time-great NBA career but enjoyed a much-too-short but successful post-playing career that included several sports-related businesses and joint ventures, including building an investment firm, acquiring 10 percent of the beverage company Bodyarmor, starting a media company called Granity Studios, and launching Mamba Sports Academy for aspiring athletes.

Of course, having made hundreds of millions of dollars and achieved celebrity status through his NBA career, Kobe certainly left the NBA with tools that the average high school graduate doesn't have at their disposal. But money, fame, and connections alone don't explain Kobe's success either during or after his NBA career. After all, how many talented basketball players never rise to the top of the NBA like Kobe did? And how many professional athletes leave their sport and end up broke just a few years later?

In other words, Kobe's success, both in the NBA and, especially, post-NBA, cannot be explained completely by talent, money, or fame alone. His mindset made him obsessed with playing bigger and better than his natural talents would typically yield. Even more importantly, however, that mindset caused him to develop habits that pushed him beyond what even the biggest, fastest, and most talented players achieved playing on the court with him. Waking up at 4 a.m. to train became his norm. And, if he was like most ultrasuccessful people in sports, business, and life, after a while, it became more uncomfortable to skip a 4 a.m. workout than to wake up and do it.

And *that's* what having billion-dollar habits looks like. It looks like programming your body, mind, and day to make success the natural outcome of what you do without thinking. It makes achieving big goals a matter of "when" not "if." It makes the work that others see as "hard" (like sending twenty-five text messages to clients, former clients, or strategic contacts every single day) or even "crazy" (like getting up at 4 a.m. to train when you're already one of the best NBA players of all time) something you barely even think about.

Having billion-dollar habits is like programming your mind and body as if you were a piece of software designed to build the momentum you need to hit your goals. You set your targets. You understand where your focus needs to be. You reverse engineer the steps it takes to work smarter, not harder. And then you start taking those steps.

At first, it feels awkward, as I'm sure it did for Kobe the first few times he woke up at 4 a.m. You're tired. You're trying new things. You might even be a little scared (or a lot) because achieving big things forces you to do different things than you are used to doing. But, as you build momentum, you'll get better and better at your new way of life and all the work you do starts becoming second nature. It becomes habitual.

Being Really Good at Being Really Good

I'm going to say something here that might be a little controversial. But that's fine. It's worth the risk of upsetting some of you to make sure I tell you the complete truth about why many of you reading this have not risen to the top of your market: most real estate agents I've met are really good at being mediocre.

That's right. They're *really* good at being mediocre.

What does that even mean? And why should you care?

Well, it means that most agents have developed habits that cap their potential way lower than it can be. They're efficient and effective at getting just enough listings to pay their bills, drive a nice car, take a nice vacation or two per year, and even save up a few bucks in their retirement account. Unfortunately, many of those agents don't realize what they're doing. They might *want* to make more money but don't believe it's possible. Some think there is something wrong with their environment that caps their income. They tell me there aren't enough listings in their neighborhood to Broker Billions. Or they tell me there is too much competition or one competitor who virtually owns the market. Or they object to the entire concept of trying innovative approaches to real estate, telling me something to the effect of

"This is how people list their homes in my area" or "All that stuff looks good on paper but won't work in the reality of real estate where I work."

If that sounds like you, you have two choices. You can close this book and go back to your normal routine. In that case, as Jessie Porter famously said, "If you always do what you've always done, you always get what you've always gotten." You will continue to be *really* good at being mediocre.

Or you can develop *new* habits that will make you *really good*. In that case, you'll likely need to get uncomfortable for a short time to try new things. You'll also need to break old habits that seemingly work because they generate mediocre results. I don't want mediocre results for you. I want you to Broker Billions. I want you to get *really good* at being *really good*.

In my first year selling real estate in Atlanta, that's exactly what I did. I set my goals. I committed to working smarter, not harder. I learned what steps it would take to get more and better listings than anyone else. And I made taking those steps so habitual I felt anxiety when I *didn't* take them.

The results: I was the top agent in Atlanta my first year. After that big splash, I could have just sat back and done the same things I did the previous year and coasted on my success. But I didn't. I set new targets for year two. I wanted to double my business and double it again and again. I developed new habits and achieved even bigger goals. I do that same exercise every year because I want to be the top broker every year. So when January 1 comes around and I'm tied for last place with every other broker and agent in Atlanta, I double down on doubling my business and developing new habits that will bring my business to even greater heights.

Why not just coast at this point? I've been asked that way too many times to count. Even when I was making $5 million selling real estate, people said, "Bonneau, you're doing great. Why would you want to change anything?" Three reasons.

First, there really isn't that big of a gap between the top agents and an average agent. The top agents are just a few small innovations ahead of the average agent. But that's all they need to be ahead. All you need to do is stay one year ahead of the average agent to Broker Billions because you'll always stand out and the average agent will always be behind.

Second, I'm obsessed with growing. That's why I started Ansley. That's why I will continue to expand it year in and year out. And that's why I've already started expanding it to other cities.

Third, when you work smarter not harder, continued growth doesn't take more work. It just takes more innovation. I'll still make it home for dinner. I'll still enjoy my family life and the hobbies I love. I'll just be making more money, helping more people, and changing the way real estate is sold around the country and beyond.

Routines: A Hidden Secret to Making Your Life Much Easier

When I asked Holly Parker what advice she would give to a newer agent or someone who wanted to go from good to great, her answer came quickly:

I would say they need a routine. They need to write down what they are committed to doing on a daily basis. And my suggestion would be that at least ninety minutes of their day should be for themselves, preferably the first ninety, setting them up for having a successful day. Get a workout, meditate, have breakfast, and write down your goals down for the day. Just doing those things repeatedly will help them tremendously. I get it. It sounds tough. Where are you going to find ninety minutes to spend on yourself? I have kids. When I decided to work on myself, I had to make time whenever I could. My kids wake up before 7:00 a.m. every day, and I also had my aging parents with me, including my mother with Alzheimer's.

But it's too important to not figure something out, even if it's hard. My solution? I woke up every single day at 5:00 a.m. It was hard, especially at first. But if I hadn't woken up and taken care of myself before I had to take care of everyone else, I would never have gotten to me. I would have spent all day taking care of other people.

Those first ninety minutes that became my oxygen. And it paid off. Not only was I more fulfilled than ever, I had tremendous sales and the Holly Parker Team was the number one team that year.

I share this part of Holly's story for two reasons. First, it demonstrates the power of habits. She made waking up at 5:00 a.m. habitual. It wasn't easy, but she was able to do it. Second, it demonstrates the power of investing in yourself.

Whether it's hiring a mentor, joining a mastermind group, signing up for a gym, or just waking up ninety minutes early for some alone time, investing in yourself can yield a tremendous return on investment—in Holly's case, making her team the number one sales team that year.

Similarly, Mark Spain swears by his morning routine to balance personal priorities with business priorities and productivity:

> I start my day, every day, the same way. I grab a cup of coffee and talk with my kids as they're eating breakfast. Then my wife and I take my kids to school together. We do this together every single day when I'm in town. When we get back home, my wife and I spend time together catching up on life and working out. Then we each go on whatever path or meetings we have.
>
> The things I talk about with my team members and what I'm trying to coach and mentor my team on is that this business is like a sport, and they are like athletes. In sports, what do athletes do? They eat healthy, work out, get a lot of sleep, and they study and read a lot. So I teach my team to make those things routine for them too. It's not about vanity. It's about keeping your head right first and your body healthy first, keeping stress level down and being healthy. You owe it to yourself and your family just to be healthy, to eat healthy, and take care of yourself.
>
> If you go listen to other successful people, most of them talk about the same because that's what's important. They're readers; their nightstands are full of books on whatever thing that you want to improve on.
>
> If you want to be successful, you've got to have a routine. You need to go to bed at the same time every day, wake up at the same time every day, work out at the same time, and do all the important business tasks—like follow-up—at the same time every day.

If you take away one thing from this chapter, it's that your routines determine a big part of your results. Routines create consistency. And what you do consistently will determine what you improve upon consistently. Make the most important parts of your day routine.

Drive + Customer Service = $100 Million (in the First Year)

When Elizabeth DeWoody started selling real estate, she didn't just dip her toe in the water and sell one or two homes. She wasn't content with being just another agent or even selling a few million a year.

In her first year, she sold about $100 million in homes. Just six years later, she sold $250 million in the high-end Palm Beach, Florida, market.

When she started, the average home she sold was about $2 million. Today, her average deal is around $5 million. Still, $100 million of sales—in her first year no less—is impressive, especially because selling homes in Palm Beach isn't simple. Even getting insurance for homes in that area is a nightmare. On top of that, Florida is full of real estate agents.

But Elizabeth was committed to helping solve all her clients' challenges to make working with her a no-brainer.

At first, she built her business with a Zillow ad, like many people do. Today, she's generating $250 million in sales mostly by referrals.

What traits does Elizabeth credit with allowing her to hit the market so strongly her first year?

"I'm a driver," says Elizabeth. "I started working in my bedroom, so I learned before the pandemic how to manage time, sell, and serve clients. You have to be honest, diligent, and service-oriented to succeed. It's hard work. It's not easy, especially in the Palm Beach market. But if you can help solve all the challenges needed to buy or sell a home, you can be successful. And if you continue your relationship with your clients beyond the sales, you can be successful for a long time."

What Separates My Brokering Billions Method from the Average Agent's Process

Although my process might not seem tremendously different from the processes many agents or brokers use, it's full of many subtle differences that have been carefully designed to separate me and my team from the two million or so real estate agents in the United States as of the time I write.

Those subtleties didn't just help me make a few extra sales here or there. They helped me become the number one broker in Atlanta. And they do the same year in and year out.

However, although those subtleties are important—we'll talk about how my process optimizes the impact of everyone on my team in the next chapter—even more important is the fact that almost every step of the process happens without anyone having to think. That's right. Everyone on my team knows exactly what needs to be done at every step in the process, who needs to do it, and how to make it happen. After all, it doesn't matter how effective a process is if nobody knows what to do it with.

That's the power of habit.

A simple but average process performed flawlessly every time will outperform a perfect but complicated process every day of the week.

Imagine, then, a simple process that leads clients through a best-in-class experience and helps match listings with buyers.

That's where agents can start to Broker Billions.

In fact, when you learn what the top brokers in the country do, you'll find that it's *easier* to Broker Billions than it is to languish in the world of average agents. You'll do less work. You'll work fewer hours. You'll make fewer mistakes. And you'll seamlessly integrate everything you need to do to Broker Billions into your life in a way that often makes it hard to tell whether you're working or playing.

For the rest of this chapter, I'm going to walk you through how to turn tasks into habits and then integrate your business activities into hobbies you love to do. Want to get listings on the golf course? With the right habits, it's easy to get listings anywhere and everywhere you go.

First Things First: What Are Habits, Exactly, and How Do They Help You Reach Your Goals?

As simple as it sounds, let's define what I mean by "habits" so we're both on the same page when it comes to turning your tasks into habits.

In short, your habits are actions you take without even thinking.

Why is that important? Two reasons.

First, it automates success throughout your team. When everyone knows what to do and instinctively performs their tasks, everyone is set up for success. Nobody needs to micromanage. No project gets stuck in the pipeline because someone doesn't know what to do next or because someone thinks another person is performing their responsibility.

Second, and even more important, they allow you to consistently raise the floor and bust through plateaus by freeing you up to always experiment and innovate. How? By breaking and replacing habits.

So let me ask you a very important question: Are your habits today on par with your dreams for tomorrow? If not, it's time for new habits. Your habits must match what you want for the future. If not, your habits will lead you somewhere else.

Habit Check: Are Your Habits Today on Par with Your Dreams for Tomorrow?

Before we continue, I want to pause on this question I just asked you to consider before we go deeper into developing Billion-Dollar habits. So, what do you think? Are your habits today on par with your dreams for tomorrow? Will continuing to do what you do every day lead you to the results you want tomorrow?

Most people's answer to this question is a resounding no. They *say* their dream is to run a marathon but they eat junk food every day and don't exercise. They *say* they want to double their sales volume but they still make the same number of cold calls, send the same number of post cards, take the same number of meetings, do the same marketing, and so forth.

The truth is you will *never* improve your results if you don't improve your habits first. If you want to get to another level of production selling real estate, you need to take your habits to another level, too.

Be Willing to Dump Your Old Habits (Even the "Good" Ones)

The old saying "Old habits die hard" couldn't be more appropriate for my journey in the real estate industry. Our habits are, according to the *Oxford Dictionary of English*, "a settled or regular tendency or practice, especially one that is hard to give up." If you have good habits, you're likely set for the marathon-like race ahead.

However, if you have bad habits, those that don't serve your goals, then you're practically living your life with an extra hundred pounds of pressure on your shoulders—and you may never get off the starting block.

Most of us have a combination of good and bad habits—we're human. These habits, whether good or bad, maintain a great deal of control over our successes or failures. Show me a remarkably flourishing entrepreneur or business owner, and I bet you'll find several strong qualities supporting him or her. But show me a fledgling or struggling business, and I imagine we can likely find several bad habits at the helm. Like it or not, your habits are often the barometer for your success.

When it comes to creating supercharged growth, I've generally found that your old habits, even some of the good ones, don't create game-changing results. It's the shift in these habits, the transformation that occurs when you decide to change the way you act, that ends up creating the most impactful results. The same practice always equals the same results. Take a lawyer, for example. Let's say they have had a fine career, and every single year they do between $2 million and $3 million worth of new business. They do the same thing every day. They do the same amount of marketing. They practice law in the same fashion. They meet with the same number of potential clients. They go on the same number of networking lunches and happy hours each year. They simply wait for the phone to ring and they go to work. Very boring, very average. But it works for them. And in the end, these practices will generate the same result.

Many people can live with average and status quo. They can exist in a world where they aren't scaling, they aren't growing. Even if they are wonderfully successful, they are complacent and hardly moving the needle. That's not for me. That's not for this book. If you are that person and want to continue to be that person, this book may not be for you. And I pass no judgment upon that. That's a good life for somebody. If you're a real estate agent doing $15 million worth of volume a year at a 3 percent commission, and the brokerage house takes home 20 percent, you're making a fairly good income. But that's not the topic of this chapter.

If old habits die hard, then this chapter on supercharged growth will help you kill them. It will support you in changing your behavior to support your growth. If ignorance is bliss, then stop reading right now. Because I'm going to challenge you in the pages ahead. Together, we're going to identify the habits that serve you and those that don't. Then, we're going to get uncomfortable. You've got to step way outside of your comfort zone and your normal modus operandi to create something special.

The truth is that it's easy to maintain and practice old habits. It's what 99 percent of us do. It's ingrained in our very existence, and in many ways, it's human nature. Human nature is hardly created to build incredible habits and allow you to dominate your field. It's human nature just to survive. So if we're going to shift our behavior to game-changing practices, we have to take the time to recognize that we're actually changing our nature, the way we're wired, and the way we approach life. While it might not happen overnight, it will happen. Incremental efforts, every single day, will eventually amount to real change that lasts. I know because I have seen it; I have done it. And if I can do it, then I know you can as well.

Breaking and Replacing Habits

In his *New York Times* best-selling book, *Moonwalking with Einstein: The Art and Science of Remembering Everything* (Penguin Books, 2011), author and journalist Joshua Foer discusses how competitors master the ability to memorize the order of a shuffled deck of cards, long strings of numbers, full original poems (punctuation and all), and more.

Among other questions, Foer sought to answer why some people can perform seemingly impossible memory feats while others routinely forget where they left their keys. Are these memory mavens just *that* much smarter than the average person? Or is there something else at play?

It turns out, there *was* something else at play, as many competitors in national and international memory competitions boasted only average intelligence. In conducting his research, Foer noticed that practice, alone, did not lead to consistent improvement beyond a certain level. This might explain, he offered, why many people who type all day at work often hit a plateau of how accurate or fast they type. If practice, alone, led to consistent improvement, people would eventually become typing masters.

One of the reasons people hit plateaus even when they work on something consistently is that their practice consists of just going through the motions. With typing, for example, some people might be content typing twenty-five words per minute, hunting and pecking on the computer to enter data into a system. They don't need to type more than twenty-five words per minute, so they never challenge themselves to try new techniques, like typing with two fingers on each hand, typing with the standard finger placement while looking at the keys, then looking away, and so forth.

In other words, people eventually stop improving because they stop breaking their habits and replacing them with better habits. Instead, they hit a plateau. To break through that plateau, you need to do two things differently, each of which results in your breaking your existing habits and replacing them with better ones: (1) tweaking your habits to consistently improve, and (2) borrowing habits from others to make giant leaps forward and shortcut your way to success.

The 1 Percent a Day Rule: Tweaking Your Habits to Consistently Improve

With his *New York Times* best-selling book, *Atomic Habits: An Easy & Proven Way to Build Good Habits & Break Bad Ones* (Avery, 2018), author James Clear did something many authors have tried and failed to do over the past several decades: introduce a take on habits that gets people's attention. Habits might be one of the most written about topics in business and personal productivity. Thus, getting people's attention with a new book about habits is no easy task.

Yet, in 2018, James Clear was able to break through all that noise and hit number one on the *New York Times* bestseller list with a simple book about habits. Since then, he's sold more than four million copies and generated more than one hundred thousand reviews on Amazon alone, with a global rating of 4.8 stars out of five.

What makes James Clear's book stand out among the thousands of other books about habits? The simplicity of both the promise and the system. In fact, it's so simple that it can be summarized in one sentence: you can get better results from the compounding effect of making a series of small changes than trying to make big changes all at once.

Clear even does the math about the compounding effect of small, incremental improvements on his website.[3] Specifically, in one year, he notes, if you become just 1 percent better every day, you'll end up 37.78 times better at the end of one year. That's not double. That's not the proverbial "10x." That's more than 37x better in just one year.

In other words, replacing your habits with new habits doesn't have to mean starting over completely. In fact, you can get huge results by simply experimenting with incremental improvements over time.

Borrowing Habits from Others to Make Giant Leaps Forward

> *"It's good to learn from your mistakes. It's better to learn from other people's mistakes."*
>
> —Warren Buffett

Just because you *can* make giant leaps by consistently improving doesn't mean you *have to* only tweak. One way I was able to double

---

3   James Clear, "How to Master the Art of Continuous Improvement," James Clear, 2015, https://jamesclear.com/continuous-improvement.

my business so many years in a row was by making big changes. But I didn't just make up the big, bold changes I made. I learned a lot of them from mentors and others who were more successful than I was, both inside and outside of real estate.

I call this strategy "borrowing habits from others." In fact, this strategy is one Joshua Foer highlights in *Moonwalking with Einstein*, as well. Specifically, in talking about how the best chess players in the world become the best of the best, Foer noted that the best chess players aren't the ones who play the most chess. Instead, they "often spend several hours a day replaying the games of grand masters one move at a time, trying to understand the expert's thinking at each step." In fact, Foer notes that "the single best predictor of an individual's chess skill is not the amount of chess he's played against opponents, but rather the amount of time he's spent sitting alone working through old games."

As counterintuitive as that might seem, the reality is that the fastest way to explosive growth is to spend time and money learning from people who have achieved what we want to achieve. From reading a book like this to listening to a podcast like the *Brokering Billions* podcast or even investing in a mentorship or mastermind program, spending time and money to learn the habits of others so you can more confidently make even bigger changes to your habits is a good investment.

The good news for you is you've already started borrowing habits from me by reading this book. The mindset and strategies I share in here cost me *a lot* of time and money. And now you can learn them for a fraction of the time and money it cost me. Invest in shortcuts to make big leaps by borrowing habits that other people have already tested.

Build On Your Strengths

If you're struggling to figure out exactly how to tweak your habits or borrow new ones, one of the best rules of thumb is to start by building on your strengths.

Dr. Edward Hallowell, who has both ADHD and dyslexia himself—and attended Harvard—is a psychiatrist who has been treating ADHD, dyslexia, and other learning differences for the past thirty-five years. His unique strength-based approach aims to "unwrap gifts rather than treat disabilities."

The "ADHD race car brain," he says, can, if managed correctly, become a major asset in your life. Dr. Hallowell says it best: "People with ADHD typically are creative, intuitive, original, and full of positive energy. They tend to be independent thinkers. They are persistent to the point of being stubborn . . . They are big-hearted and generous. They often have charisma or a special something, a twinkle in the eye, a zany sense of humor, or an ability to inspire others. With the right kind of guidance, these people can become hugely successful in their lives."[4]

To take this even further, he outlines the seven habits of highly effective ADHD adults. These include

1. Do what you're good at. Don't spend too much time trying to get good at what you're bad at. (You did enough of that in school.)
2. Delegate what you're bad at to others, as often as possible.

---

4   Kathy Salas, "Top 10 Questions on ADHD by Edward M. Hallowell," Kathy Salas, February 18, 2014, https://kathysalas.com/adhd/adhd-articles/top-10-questions-on-adhd-by-edward-m-hallowell/.

3. Connect your energy to a creative outlet.
4. Get well-enough organized to achieve your goals. The key here is "well-enough." That doesn't mean you have to be well organized at all—just well-enough organized to achieve your goals.
5. Ask for and heed advice from people you trust—and ignore, as best you can, the dream-breakers and finger-waggers.
6. Make sure you keep up regular contact with a few close friends.
7. Go with your positive side. Even though you have a negative side, make decisions and run your life with your positive side.

This is a blueprint for ADHD/dyslexic people to turn supposed weaknesses into strengths, and over the years, it has reminded me how I can turn my perceived weaknesses into extraordinary strengths.

I regularly delegate, focus on my strengths, remain organized, make it a priority to keep up with friends, and always trust in my team. I didn't always do that. It took some time for me to fully relinquish control to team members, but I now attribute a great deal of our quick growth to my full investment in their abilities.

Make Your Actual Weaknesses Less Relevant

While Dr. Hallowell wrote this list for those of us with ADHD/ dyslexia, it applies to us all, no matter what our limitations may be. You may not be impacted by learning disabilities like I am, but each and every one of us has weaknesses.

In that vein, one of the habits Dr. Hallowell put on his list was to delegate what you're bad at to others as often as possible. While this is certainly a trait of highly effective ADHD adults, it's also worth trying to minimize what you're bad at in the first place. If you focus on building on your weaknesses, you have a larger arsenal of strengths and fewer holes in your bucket.

So here is what I want you to do:

1. Put your list of weaknesses or limitations in front of you.
2. Number them.
3. Next to each one, take the time to brainstorm and write out an example of how you can leverage this weakness and improve upon it, eliminate it from needing to be done completely, or delegate it to someone else who is strong in that task. This is where it starts to get interesting.

Through the years, I've not only recognized my weaknesses but I've also put a plan of action in place to transform them into team strengths by delegating them to others. I have worked hard over the years to minimize those areas in which I had to improve.

That's not to say I don't still have issues or areas I want to continue to develop—that's a lifelong journey for us all. But I have secured enough progress so that my weaknesses aren't all that weak anymore and have hired strong people to backfill. In this way, I've effectively recognized supercharged growth.

Within just one year of adding my integral team members to free up my time, I went from $100 million in sales to $175 million, a 75 percent increase. Who wouldn't be happy with that? Had I just followed my path of focusing on strengths, I would have remained stagnant. But turning weaknesses into strengths allowed me to almost double my business in just a year.

Does that sound exciting to you? It should, but the process will not be without effort and energy. The definition of insanity is doing the same thing again and again and expecting different results. Only when we actively analyze, evaluate, and then focus on our weaknesses can we ultimately build something amazing. If you want supercharged growth, then it's up to you, and only you, to leverage those limitations.

Make Your Habits Self-Serving

My goal with this book is to help you create amazing habits that serve you and support your growth, both in your personal life and your business. Like Benjamin Franklin said, "It is easier to prevent bad habits than to break them." We get comfortable in our habits. Why wouldn't we? Many of them have been with us since virtually the beginning of our lives. We are born with innate tendencies and inclinations. But in some sense, that's what makes it so challenging to break habits in the first place. As Russell Poldrack, a professor of psychology at Stanford University, says, "We want the brain to learn how to do those things without energy and effort. Habits are an adaptive feature of how the brain works."[5]

"We are action-oriented creatures," says Elliot Berkman, director of the University of Oregon's Social and Affective Neuroscience Lab. In fact, studies have shown you are more likely to think of what you are suppressing the more you try to suppress it. One study found that some people even exhibit a behavioral rebound effect, where they do more of what they tried to avoid, for example.

---

5   Cassie Shortsleeve, "5 Science-Approved Ways to Break a Bad Habit," *Time*, August 28, 2018, https://time.com/5373528/break-bad-habit-science/.

My point in sharing this with you is to help you understand three things:

1. Your habits are extremely powerful forces in your life.
2. It is easier to form new positive habits than to break old ones.
3. The more energy you give your bad habits (whether in a good or a bad way), the more prevalent they will be in your life.

I learned early in my career that my habits would define my success. No ifs, ands, or buts. There is a powerful connection between what you do and what you achieve. In my business of residential real estate, I decided early on I wanted to be present everywhere and be part of the movement and story. When I meet someone new and we're chatting, I tastefully bake in the fact that I sell real estate.

And that's why I advertise so much bigger than everybody else. Early on, I created the habit of always outadvertising my competition. If somebody takes out a quarter-page ad in a local real estate newspaper, I'll take out a full-page, and then I'll make sure it reaches every single relevant neighborhood; I'll send out not just a normal postcard, but an oversized postcard, often legal size that can't even fit in their mailbox. The postman has to fold it to get it to fit. And then I'll hit them again a month later with a different postcard, also oversized. I'm not trying to annoy potential clients. Rather, I'm trying to engage with them in a different way, a habit I formed early in my career.

There's so much noise in this world, and you've got to figure out how to be unique and how to form habits that are different from everyone else's—even when you're starting your business. I was fortunate enough that I found the confidence to act like I was the number one realtor in Atlanta long before I was number one. I always had a house to show. When I would meet somebody, I'd immediately say, "I've got the perfect house for you." And then I'd go back to the office and research the market to find that perfect home.

You never know where your new habits and techniques will take you. My son's school regularly hosts career day. Each week, a mom or dad comes to the kids' class and talks about what they do for work. When I came into my son's fifth-grade class, I brought a bunch of Ansley Atlanta T-shirts and one of my print marketing materials with home listings, *The Ansley Paper.*

I told them about my life selling houses and gave everybody a T-shirt when they asked me good questions. And then I gave them all *The Ansley Paper* and said, "Everybody pick out your favorite house in here and draw a heart around it and take it home to your parents." And by doing that, they came home wearing my Ansley Atlanta T-shirt, with *The Ansley Paper* with their favorite house circled, and with an understanding of how the selling process goes. I gained more clients from that career day at my son's school than I have through many other presentations I've done. Even an elementary school "career day" is an opportunity to completely slay it.

Chapter 5:

Building Your Dedicated and High-Functioning Team to Perform the Tasks You Shouldn't Be Doing

"A lot of real estate agents like a side hustle. I tried driving Uber, but I couldn't fit my passengers in the back of my Ferrari."

—Yours Truly, Atlanta's "Funniest" Real Estate Agent

Bill Belichick is the long-tenured coach of the New England Patriots. Widely considered one of the greatest coaches in NFL history, he has won six Super Bowl titles. He has greater than a 65 percent win percentage and ranks first in NFL coaching history with more than 300 wins, including the playoffs. His team has had a winning record in eighteen consecutive seasons and is known to be relentless in its preparation. But even more interesting is Belichick's game plan.

In preparation for an NFL Sunday, his team practices all week to accomplish two things:

1. Take away the greatest strength of their opponent.
2. Do all the small things well.

For example, if the Patriots are playing a team with a great running game, they'll focus on stopping the run. The same is true if they run into a gun-slinging quarterback. The Patriots come up with a truly unique game plan specifically designed to counteract what their opponents' strengths and weaknesses are, each and every week. This is their system; it's what they do. Belichick takes away whatever it is that makes the opposition successful.

They also spend a lot of time mastering the small details of each position. Each player becomes an expert at the fundamentals of their position, famously touting the team's mantra of having each player simply "do their job." From footwork to route running, hand positioning, clock management, and everything in between, the Patriots are known to be disciplined in all the little things that make football players succeed.

It works. Why? Well, because Belichick understands how to build a team that can thrive in any environment. He knows if he removes the strength of another team, then all that will remain will be some form of weakness. Left with a weak running or passing game, the Patriots' opponent will have to try to beat them by trying to use a weakness.

Unlike many other teams, which play one consistent style of offense or defense, it's not uncommon for Belichick's team to play zone defense one week and man-to-man defense another, depending on their strengths, the other team's strengths and weaknesses, and even the field conditions. In fact, in a December 6, 2021, game against the Buffalo Bills that featured wind gusts over forty miles per hour, the Patriots threw only three times all game, running for 222 yards on forty-six carries.

Belichick builds his team to be adaptable and able to compete under virtually any conditions. He values versatility over raw talent, leadership skills over individual performance, and mental toughness over pure physical capabilities. He puts his money where his mouth is, too, often taking draft picks or making trades that leave people scratching their heads.

But his success on the field speaks for itself, starting by drafting Tom Brady in the sixth round, keeping him on a roster that already had three quarterbacks, and giving him the opportunity to start in place of the veteran starter Drew Bledsoe as the veteran recovered from the injury that forced Brady into duty two games into the 2001 season. It didn't matter that Bledsoe had signed the biggest contract in NFL history, a ten-year, $103 million deal, mere months earlier, which the Associated Press described as "virtually guarantee[ing] he will spend his entire career with the New England Patriots."[6] Tom Brady had proven he was the best quarterback for the team, even if he wasn't yet the better quarterback of the two. So Brady started, Bledsoe was eventually traded within the division to the aforementioned Buffalo Bills for a first-round draft pick, and the rest is history.

---

6   "PLUS: N.F.L.; Richest Contract Goes to Bledsoe," *New York Times*, March 8, 2001, Sports, https://www.nytimes.com/2001/03/08/sports/plus-nfl-richest-contract-goes-to-bledsoe.html.

If you ask Belichick about the key to his success, he will inevitably give credit to his players, coaches who support him, and their collective commitment to playing as a high-functioning team.

Your strengths will dictate your floor, but building a team to turn your personal weaknesses into team strengths will allow you to surpass your ceilings over and over again.

Just like in football, building a team that accentuates your strengths, overcomes your weaknesses, and adapts to what you need to do to succeed in any environment is the secret to long-term growth. Specifically, just like any team can win one game on any given Sunday, any team can sell a house or two, especially in favorable environments.

But if you want consistent success, like the twenty-plus year run of success the Patriots achieved from 2001 through at least the 2021–2022 season when they reached the playoffs with rookie Mac Jones as their quarterback, you need to build a dedicated and high-functioning team you can rely on to do the tasks you shouldn't be doing, adapt to changing circumstances, and even take over some of the tasks that don't *need* to be done by you.

I want you to walk in Belichick's shoes for just a second. Go back to your numbered list of limitations or weaknesses you created at the end of the last chapter.

Imagine you're playing against Bill Belichick and *know* he is going to do everything he can to take away your strengths and force you to spend most of your time on your weaknesses. For this purpose, forget your ability to rely on your gut, innovation, or execution skills. Belichick game-planned for you and has made sure that everybody on his team does something very, very well to counter whatever you can do to adjust. You *must* win by doing what you do *worst*.

What do you do?

If you have a team in place that excels where you don't, your response is simple: you put your team in and they start to excel. At that point, Belichick has a choice: he can change his game plan to defend against what you do well, in which case you will start to crush him by working in your areas of strength, or he can stick with his game plan to avoid going directly against you, personally, and hope your team wears down.

How Game Planning and Team Building Work in the Real Estate World

Although the football example might seem a little detached from the real estate world, I spend a lot of time game planning, playing to my strengths, and improving, delegating, or eliminating tasks I'm weak in.

For example, let's say there's a house that hasn't sold with another agency and the listing is getting ready to expire. I watch these listings like a hawk and want to take them over the second the existing contract expires.

I might get a call from the seller or may call him myself. In my pitch, I'll say, "Look, we've got the same house to sell and we're in the same market. Let's talk about what I can do differently from your current agent to get this house sold."

I'll ask the seller what their agent did well and what they did not do well. In that way, I can understand the dynamic of what they're looking for and can try to backfill where the other agent might have failed. I don't want to repeat what the other person did and have the house not sell, so having that information is critical. I want to build a different game plan for the property and put the right mix of people from my team whose strengths fit the customized game plan.

Then, with the new game plan and mix of team members in place, I'll get to work. My team and I might change the orientation of the pictures on the house's web page. If the pictures are heavy on the interior, I might go heavier on the exterior, focusing on their beautiful property. I might tell them that we need to do some staging or paint a couple of rooms to freshen them up. I might propose some ideas to target a different demographic than the first listing to attract new potential buyers to the house. I make a solid marketing plan and make sure I have buy-in from the seller.

This is just one way that having a versatile, high-functioning team sets you up to Broker Billions and is exactly what Bill Belichick does on the playing field. If a team struggled against the run throughout the season, he'll build more run plays and put more run protectors in the lineup. If the opposing defense adjusts and starts thwarting the run, he'll put more play action in place, faking the run before hitting receivers with passes to take advantage of the defense biting on the fake run play.

In Belichick's words, "There is an old saying about the strength of the wolf is the pack, and I think there is a lot of truth to that. On a football team, it's not the strength of the individual players, but it is the strength of the unit and how they all function together. We'll continue to work hard to do a better job in every area going forward. I don't know where those little things will come from but we'll continue to be diligent on them."

And this has worked for Belichick and his teams for more than two decades, and even after losing the most successful quarterback in the history of the NFL to the Tampa Bay Buccaneers. Great team builders have people in place who can focus on a million different things to ensure they have a leg up on the competition. Their teams understand how to adapt to situations; they rarely make mistakes, miss blocks, throw interceptions, or turn the ball over. They're consistent, resilient, and rarely make unforced errors. They fight for every advantage, limit and leverage their own limitations, and do all the small things well.

As Al Pacino said in the movie *Any Given Sunday*, "On this team we fight for that inch. On this team we tear ourselves and everyone else around us to pieces for that inch. We claw with our fingernails for that inch. Because we know when we add up all those inches, that's gonna make the F****** difference between WINNING and LOSING, between LIVING and DYING! I'll tell you this, in any fight it's the guy who's willing to die who's gonna win that inch."

The heavy hitters know they won't win the game on their strengths, but rather they will win it on reshaping their weaknesses into something that can actually serve them at a higher level. That's where we find the inches.

With that context in place, here's the recipe I use to build a team that consistently outperforms the competition.

The Team That Gets You to the Top of the Top

As I mentioned earlier, Mark Spain and his team at Mark Spain Real Estate sold more than $3.3 billion in residential real estate and served more than 10,300 clients in 2021. How good is that? It was good enough for his team to be named the number one real estate team for closed transactions in the US by the *Wall Street Journal*, a feat they've achieved for five consecutive years.

What's the secret to their success? Team.

Be Smart Enough to Know How Dumb You Are

> *"Everybody is a genius. But if you judge a fish by its ability to climb a tree, it will live its whole life believing that it is stupid."*
>
> —Unknown

In the world of social media, many quotes get misattributed or attributed to multiple people. Such is the case with this quote about identifying everyone's genius. The quote is most frequently attributed to Albert Einstein, who would know a thing or two about being a genius, but some people dispute that Einstein actually said this quote.

Regardless of who said it first, the point it makes goes to the core of building a team that allows you to focus most of your time on your strengths while strategically strengthening areas of weakness.

Specifically, one of the hardest lessons many brokers and agents learn is that it takes dozens of tasks to Broker Billions, and they are probably only truly experts at a handful of those tasks. Many times, they have worked hard as solo agents or team members—many times outworking the competition, as opposed to outsmarting them. Of those who do outsmart the competition, many of them *also* outwork them.

While outworking people can build *some* level of success, especially when combined with outsmarting them, relying on outworking people to maintain your level of success is a recipe for burnout. Eventually, you'll crash and burn.

When I got started, I was fortunate to have been battling my supposed "weaknesses" of ADHD and dyslexia for as long as I could remember. I faced challenges every single day just trying to stay focused.

It didn't take long for me to learn I *can't* and *shouldn't* do everything that's needed to Broker Billions because I'm not the right person for everything. I'm probably good at 10 percent of the stuff I do on my team side, and I'm probably only good at 10 percent of the stuff we do as a company at Ansley | Christie's International Real Estate.

I'm smart enough to know how dumb I am.

Yes, I know being less talented at something doesn't mean you or I are dumb. But my point is that I'm either the right or wrong person to be performing tasks. I focus my time on the 10 percent of tasks I'm good at and enjoy, and I delegate, automate, or outsource the other tasks.

Let's do the math there. If you can go from doing 100 percent of the tasks to just 10 percent with the other 90 percent being performed by other people who excel in those tasks, you can get the same amount of work done while cutting your workday by 90 percent. Or you can 10x your volume while working the same hours. For most people, the right mix is somewhere in the middle.

As I built Ansley | Christie's International Real Estate from the ground up, I quickly realized that I needed the help and support of others to create a strong infrastructure along the way. There was no way I could have built the culture we have today on my own, the remarkable processes and tech we have in place, or even the team that goes to work and reps the Ansley brand every single day. I knew, early on, that to do this, I needed the support of others.

On average over the last seven years, my team has gone from $100 million in production to over $450 million per year. I've got five people on my team, and with them, I've been able to successfully backfill things I am not as good at with people who are highly efficient and effective in those areas.

Even from the beginning of my career in real estate at a young age, I realized that you can hire to fill the gaps in your own skill set. You don't have to necessarily improve on every one of your weaknesses. Rather, you win the race of business if you can determine each weakness and then hire strong team members in these areas. That has been one of the most thoughtful and helpful steps I've taken over the years. I recognize what I am good at, like generating business and closing deals, and spend my time doing just that. I've been able to recognize where I was lacking or where my time was not best spent and then hire to fill in the gaps.

To put even more of the picture together about my team, I want to introduce you to two key members, Hil Harper and Julie Harris.

Meet Hil Harper

It was kind of fate when I met Hil Harper eleven years ago. He was my first hire at my old firm. A client of mine introduced us. Hil loved real estate, had good style and an appreciation for the finer things in life, and wanted to move from Cartersville, Georgia, to Atlanta.

The first time we met, I saw a good-looking, fit guy, who clearly played the part. He was engaging and always looked you in the eye. I thought he was professional, and that he could represent me well. I hired Hil, and he hit the ground running. Because I can't be everywhere at once, I gradually released control and leveraged Hil to work on my behalf with many of my clients. Releasing control is one of the hardest things for an agent to do, but it's the only way to scale.

We agreed to offer Hil a percentage of the houses he listed, and even now he surpasses every goal we set. But perhaps what I value most about Hil is his loyalty. His first year he earned around $30K, and now he consistently makes over $1 million.

It works the same way with our clients. There are some who I think might work well with Hil, so I have him take the lead on those. Then there are some where I might be the better lead. That's why our partnership works. It makes our jobs fun, and it's a good team that we've put together.

"I'm very structured. I'm at the office every morning and at the end of every day. During the day, I'm out taking on listings or selling people homes. No day is the same because it's really not a routine-type job. I am in charge of overseeing our team, focusing on buyers and listings—and then managing those from start to finish on most days. Bonneau and I are yin and yang, and that's why it works—we balance each other out. He's very relaxed in many ways, and he's also very approachable as a leader. It's been a privilege to collaborate with him over the past decade."

—Hil Harper

Meet Julie Harris

I first met Julie Harris in 2009 at my old firm. At the time, she was the marketing director and had been with the firm for thirteen years. I met her on my first day on the job. I walked in the front door, and she was one of the first people I saw. The first thing out of my mouth, as a rookie agent, was "I'm going to be the top agent in Atlanta this year." She looked at me and didn't bat an eye. She said, "Well, if you're going to do that, you're going to need to have a marketing plan. Let me help you with that." I felt like she had total confidence in me from day one.

When I started my business, I had a one-year noncompete agreement with my old firm. When that lapsed, Julie was the first call I made. We had developed a wonderful friendship through the years, and I knew she wasn't fulfilled or challenged in her job. She had an incredible career ahead of her, and I wanted to give her a road map so that she could achieve everything she wanted to do in her life. I challenged her to leave her brokerage firm to start a new venture with me, to get out of her comfort zone, because I knew she could do so much more than she was doing. She could run with my culture and brand, and be the person to relate to and talk to our agents.

So, together, we created a position for her as the chief people officer. The idea was that if people are the lifeblood of the organization, they need a mentor, a steadfast leader, someone on whom they can rely and lean on to help them exhibit and carry the Ansley brand. We also knew that the marketing piece was critical. There was room for improvement in our industry, and she was given full freedom to create the vision and team she wanted. She believed in me, never wavered, and came on over.

Drawing on a twenty-year career in real estate, Julie has worked across disciplines, including years as an agent assistant, which allowed her to learn in a "boots-on-the-ground" kind of way what an agent really does. She then got her sales license and expanded her portfolio to marketing and creative, and finally, served in a leadership role as assistant sales manager at our old firm.

Julie's responsibilities at Ansley | Christie's International Real Estate center on furthering our growth through shaping the company's vision, culture, and creative. These things may seem like different roles, but they are entwined and all work together to promote great success. Her experience and creative vision translate into a real-world understanding of the business from multiple vantage points—the agent, the staff, the buyer and seller, and most importantly, how they work together. With her broad skill set, Julie collaborates in all areas of Ansley to leverage insight, ideas, data, and needs.

Having a Team Allows You to Focus On What You Do Best

Hil and Julie have been true gifts, allowing me to focus my time on other areas of our business. That's been one of the most important aspects of our team's growth. Sometimes a client will tell me, "I want just you." I then explain to them that they don't want only me because I'm not good at everything. I tell them they've got to trust the system I've created because it has proven results over the past decade. Setting up clear expectations with the client is a critical function.

It would have been much harder to try to do it all on my own. I would have been miserable and would have hit a thousand different roadblocks. But I recognized early on that there are only so many hours in the day. I learned from experience that when I tried to do it all on my own, I ended up being spread too thin and needed help in getting everything done. I realized that my team could help me scale.

In that capacity, I was very thoughtful about my hires. I always found team members that filled in a gap for me. I didn't necessarily need a bunch more Bonneaus. What I needed were people who could help me turn my weaknesses into strengths. I needed folks with alternative skill sets. It wouldn't make a lot of sense to hire people with the same skills. This would not only be a cardinal sin in the book of supercharged growth it would also create a strange dynamic.

Strong leaders are often those who identify their limitations and work to offset the impact of those constraints. Teddy Roosevelt said, "The best executive is the one who has sense enough to pick good men to do what he wants done, and self-restraint enough to keep from meddling with them while they do it."

Moving forward, you must recognize and practice gap-filling.

Finding the Ying to Your Yang (or Your "Wing" to Your "Wong")

Although much of this chapter focuses on finding team members to support you, another approach to team building involves finding key strategic partners for your business.

For example, when I decided to create *Brokering Billions*, I brought in Chris Tuff as a partner. Chris is an amazing guy. He's the best-selling author of two books. In 2019, he published *The Millennial Whisperer: The Practical, Profit-Focused Playbook for Working with and Motivating the World's Largest Generation* (Morgan James Publishing, 2019), which provides research-based and real-world tested strategies for building highly productive intergenerational relationships in the workplace.

Three years later, he published his latest book, *Save Your Asks: Evolve Your Networking Currencies. Grow Your Influence. Triple Your Business.* (Panta Press, 2022), which teaches people how to build more and deeper business relationships.

I first met Chris because of *The Millennial Whisperer*, which I found incredibly valuable in building my team over the last few years. And when he shared an early draft of *Save Your Asks* with me, I *knew* Chris was someone I needed to partner with if I wanted to make *Brokering Billions* the best it could be.

After publishing his first book, Chris was brought in to help improve the mindset, systems, and processes at some of the most successful companies in the world, such as Nike, Cox Enterprises, and the Home Depot. He's also helped smaller businesses that were serious about growing.

Chris knows how to turn content into training programs that help people get results. Because that's what I wanted to do with *Brokering Billions*, I knew Chris would be the perfect person to partner with if I wanted to really help agents grow.

I use the same approach in real estate, too, such as when I partnered with Thad Wong and Mike Golden to expand Ansley Real Estate through Christie's International Real Estate. I had met Thad and quickly realized what he and Mike could bring to the table perfectly complemented what I had built.

The more I got to know Thad and Mike, the more I realized their partnership represented an incredible example of two very different people getting together to make each of them more successful. What I observed was that, although they are both professional and productive, Thad is more of a creative guy and Mike is more of the other side of the business.

When interviewing Thad for this book, I asked him to describe how he and Mike offset each other's weaknesses and round out the talents at the top of their organizations:

> First of all, we call it 'wing and wong. Mike's the wing and I'm the wong. But we are two incredibly different people. We come from different places. We're interested in incredibly different things. Our wives are incredibly different women. We'd have never been friends in high school. He would have always wanted to date my girlfriends, and I would always be stealing his trombone.
>
> The truth is, if you met Mike and me, you would not likely understand our friendship. And that's the beauty of it. Even though we are incredibly different people, we value each other equally. And even though we have incredibly different talents, we value those talents even more than our own talents because we can't do what the other does. And that's hard.
>
> A lot of times, with partnerships, things like ego, finances, and romance breaks partners apart. And for our relationship, where we've been partners for more than twenty-five years, we've been through ups, we've been through downs.
>
> But two things keep us together and working well. First, we have an incredible amount of trust. Ours is the most

trusting relationship you'll ever find. We don't even have a contract. We have a handshake and a hug.

Second, we have a tremendous amount of acceptance for each other. We both know and accept that each one of us is doing the absolute best we can do for what we are focused on achieving. Once you know someone's doing their best, if they win or fail, it's okay because you knew they gave it their all.

It's almost like the exact same qualities you want in a good marriage, trust, and acceptance. And that's what we have. We don't have to be the same. We don't believe the same things. But we have a foundation of valuing the other as much, if not more than, we value ourselves.

When Thad and I first started talking, we both noticed a similar quality between us. As Thad describes it, "We are very different guys from very different places, families, ideas, very different beliefs. But we have some core values, which are very important, such as our honor, our integrity, our service, and our relationships. Those are the consistent core values in human beings that are far more important than the extra stuff, the fanfare."

This mutual respect and admiration for each other helps in so many ways. For example, Thad reminded me of a situation we had where we were not on the same page about something. I reached out to him to have an open conversation to get us both on the same page. For some partnerships, this type of conversation could have been uncomfortable, or worse. However, our conversation *deepened* our relationship because it allowed both of us to demonstrate our mutual respect.

Using Partnerships to Achieve More Than "Just" Higher Production

I've been friends with Keene Reese since I was ten years old. He and I would eventually work together at Palmetto Bluff, the developer-owned community I mentioned in the introduction. Keene is now a partner with Johnny Ussery at the Ussery Group in Bluffton, South Carolina.

Back then, however, Keene was working long hours, had limited earning potential, and was basically running in a hamster wheel selling property at Palmetto Bluff. If you've never worked for a developer-owned community before, it brings with it several unique elements, such as only being able to sell developer-owned properties and, sometimes, resales within that development. On top of that, property values are limited to what the development can fetch on the market. You can't branch out to other neighborhoods or towns with higher price points.

You might think the limited number of properties makes for a lifestyle-friendly job. Unfortunately, it's often the opposite. You're often churning and burning, especially when new releases hit the market and you have a lot of properties you need to move.

It's a tough position to be in if you want a great work-life balance. When Keene was selling for Palmetto Bluff, he'd often work 8:00 a.m. to 5:00 or 6:00 p.m., but his phone would ring well past quitting time.

I remember having multiple conversations with Keene talking about his job. Keene has a strong work ethic, so his natural tendency is to put his head down and work. But, over time, that's a recipe for misery.

Keene worked at Palmetto Bluff for eighteen years, working both in development and in real estate sales, eventually selling close to $200 million of properties. When he joined the Ussery Group, Keene was able to achieve multiple goals. Most notably, however, was the ability to use his relationships with his partners to achieve a lifestyle balance that allows him to be much more present with his wife and three kids.

As Keene puts it:

There's one way to be completely burned out in this business is to be working seven days a week for ten years. And when I say seven days a week for ten years, that's what I was doing. I was working every day in that office and not doing anything. I wasn't going out, going to baseball tournaments, playing with my daughters, or hanging out with my wife, like I should. I wasn't seeing friends or doing really anything that helped me become more fulfilled.

At Ussery Group, we still work hard. I mean, that's just what we do. But having partners who are equally committed to each other and our clients allows all of us to be much more flexible with our schedules.

Before, I'd sometimes have to leave church in the middle of a sermon to go to the office, where I'd work until six in the evening, or later. Having partners like those at the Ussery Group has helped me and my family quite a bit, all without sacrificing how much success we have as a company and our ability to serve our clients well.

To be clear, we all still work hard. But we're much more flexible. I'm home much more often. I get to go places I want. I get to be with my family. And I have all the devices that allow me to be more flexible. I get much more freedom.

As Keene's experience shows, bringing the right partners in can achieve many goals. Yes, like Thad and Mike, partners can provide complementary skills. But the right partners can do much more than increase production. They can also increase your fulfillment, allowing you and your family to enjoy lifestyle benefits that might otherwise be tough to achieve alone.

The Anatomy of a High-Functioning Team

Julie Faupel sells real estate in Jackson Hole, Wyoming. But she doesn't *just* sell real estate in Jackson Hole, Wyoming. She sells *a lot* of real estate in Jackson Hole, Wyoming.

In 2021 alone, she sold about sixty homes for total sales of $327 million. She's the founder and CEO of REALM, an invitation-only group of real estate professionals that includes a patented technology platform that allows her agents to get industry-leading data.

Clearly, July knows something about Brokering Billions.

Selling that volume isn't without its challenges though. "Inventory has become so constrained, we're looking everywhere we possibly can to get listings and sell homes," Julie says. "In fact, we set a record in 2021, having sold a $65 million home, which was more than double the next single-family residential sale that had ever happened in the market."

As you might imagine, Julie doesn't move that volume of real estate alone. Like most agents who Broker Billions, she has incredible support, both from mentorships and a dedicated team that includes four founding partners/associate brokers, an additional associate broker, a sales associate and contract coordinator, and a marketing manager. In her words:

One of the things we always are looking at is the succession plan within the team. We have another member of our team who is coming up through the ranks being part of the partnership. We consider her part of the future of the team. We're constantly cultivating new talent.

We also have an incredible support team, including the contracts coordinator, the transaction coordinator, the marketing manager. We also have a person who is a bit of a "catch all" for everything else.

Our approach to team building is that it's more about putting things together that complement our skill sets. But also, we look at what stage our team is in as we move along and evolve to make sure we have a strong succession plan and our team members are well taken care of and receive the best training possible so they can achieve their own career goals. For example, one thing I'm very proud of is that we have had a number of people who have left our team and built very successful individual real estate careers. So we've always looked at it pretty holistically, like how do we best foster everybody's success and capitalize on those strengths as well as the needs of the team? And, when we do that, everyone tends to benefit.

One thing I love about Julie's approach to team building is that it leads to people staying because they *want* to, not because they *have* to. She gives them all the tools they need to be successful, and some of those people move on and do different things. That's fine.

The last thing you want is for someone to stay on your team because they need a paycheck. Those people bring your culture down. They bring your energy down. And they can destroy your team from the inside out.

A Strong Company Culture Is Key to Growth

Before growing your team, make sure you have a strong company culture in place. Otherwise, you could spend countless hours and money attracting the most talented and experienced team members only to have them leave before they once have a look behind the scenes at your company.

That's because the best team members have options. Unless they're related to you, they won't stick around long if your culture is toxic.

Fortunately, when I left my old firm, my one-year noncompete gave me the time to focus on building such a strong culture that it was easy for Julie to say yes to me when I called her to join me.

Thus, while it might seem natural to want to hire a bunch of people to take tasks off your plate, avoid the urge to skip over evaluating your company culture to make sure it's ready. You might not have the benefit/burden of a one-year noncompete to legally prevent you from bringing in the team members you desire, but you can still take *some* time to decide what culture you want to build from this point forward.

A strong cultural identity separates the winners from the losers, the front runners from the bottom feeders, and happy workplaces from miserable ones. I'm proud of the culture we've built at Ansley | Christie's International Real Estate, and I know that culture has been one of the greatest catalysts for our success.

Culture is like gas on a fire. It's an accelerant that can take you to the next level. That's what I want for you: supercharged growth through supercharged culture.

Follow the steps in this chapter and you will find yourself in a great position to create a contagious culture that will manifest itself throughout your business and generate more success and positive outcomes than you could ever imagine.

Creating a Contagious Culture

Every step, decision, or implementable that you take on should be for the sole purpose of crafting a contagious culture. People want to be around us at Ansley because we religiously focus on creating a contagious culture. And we're constantly working to reinvent, reinvigorate, and recharge our company. I refuse to settle for anything less than the best culture we can create. Mark Parker, CEO of Nike, said, "We have a culture where we are incredibly self-critical; we don't get comfortable with our success." I feel as if we have a similar attitude at Ansley. It would be easy to say, "We are good." But the truth is that the competition is always coming at us. They aren't going to stop, and neither are we. If we aren't evolving, then we're going to die. When you work in any highly competitive environment, it's your people that are the difference. And happy team members are the most empowered to produce remarkable results.

Paul Orfalea, founder of Kinko's, wrote a book that has really inspired me: *Copy This!: Lessons from a Hyperactive Dyslexic who Turned a Bright Idea Into One of America's Best Companies* (Workman Publishing, 2005). The book tells his story of a childhood spotted with no fewer than eight school failures. I can relate. But he eventually grew up to found and grow a great company that has been repeatedly named by *Fortune* as one of the best places to work, later selling to FedEx for $2.2 billion in cash plus the assumption of $200 million in debt.[7]

---

7   Rick Brooks, "FedEx to Buy Kinko's for $2.2 Billion," *Wall Street Journal*, December 31, 2003, News, https://www.wsj.com/articles/ SB107278969871498900.

All through school, Paul struggled to read; he struggled to write. Consequently, he became a goof-off. I see so much of my own temperament and management style in his story. But more than anything, I identify with the fact that Paul, when he decided to start his own copy business close to a university, knew he had to create a positive, cheerful, uplifting culture not only for his customers but for his coworkers in order to succeed. That's what we shoot for at Ansley. We want agents who can't wait to get to the office to interact with their fellow team members. If we live real estate, it's important that we live it together.

Orfalea said, "I knew our coworkers would be stronger in teams than on their own . . . This is only one of the many gifts of my 'disorders,' all of which contributed enormously to the building of both Kinko's and of my life. They propelled me to think differently. They forced me to rely on other people. I was prevented from taking inspiration from books; I had to learn from the world itself, directly. I had to rely on my own eyes, a skill not enough people make use of these days. My 'disabilities' enabled me to focus on the big picture at Kinko's, something I call being 'on' your business instead of 'in' it. Being 'on' your business and your life means having enough detachment every day that you are constantly reassessing your direction, thinking creatively about your overall strategy, and scrutinizing your competitors' tactics. It means relying on others to attend to most of the details of the day-to-day operations and employing a system of checks to verify that you are on the right track."

Orfalea observed that many of his customers came in anxious, rushed, and stressed about getting their projects copied and organized. The store environment and the calmness and efficiency of his coworkers could do a lot to calm his customers and assure them that their projects would be completed accurately and on time. We feel the same way at Ansley. We're assisting people in making the single largest and likely most important purchase or sale of their lives. We have to do all we can to reduce their stress and create a comfortable process in an otherwise uncomfortable scenario. It isn't easy, but if we align our culture and all work together, then we absolutely can achieve this lofty goal.

I carefully consider daily how we can make minor tweaks to improve our culture and constantly keep it on point. Why? Because I know firsthand that is where you either succeed or fail. It's so easy to see that contagious culture creates happy teams that drive hard for success. That's why I rarely, if ever, stop talking about culture at Ansley. I constantly meet with senior leadership to find out what works and what doesn't. Orfalea said, "It wasn't the task of copy making that attracted [my staff] to Kinko's, obviously. It was the culture, the feel of the place." We recognize that at Ansley, and so we do everything we can to instill that same attitude in our team and throughout our organization. And as we continue our race toward constantly building a culture that lasts, I'm going to outline some of the steps we've taken as a company to ratchet it up to the next level.

Mentor Up and Mentor Down

Rob Thomson's real estate company has about eighty agents and does about $1 billion a year in business. He has a title company and an insurance, mortgage, and brokerage company, and a bunch of affiliate companies that go with it. How does he keep it all functioning so smoothly?

"My mother taught me a whole lot," says Rob, who notes that his mother, who is in her nineties, still works at his company. "She reads every contract we write, and she's still very involved on multiple levels."

"One of the lessons my mother taught me was the value of mentorship at all levels of a company," Rob explains. "Typically, when you think of mentorship, you think of someone more experienced than you. While that's very important because that experience is tremendously valuable, we need to understand that experienced agents can learn a lot from newer agents and support team members too."

As Rob describes it, be willing to "mentor up and mentor down" in your organization. Encourage everyone to get input from people less experienced than they are. Sometimes, a fresh perspective that's not burdened by how something has been done for twenty years is just what you need to break away from the competition.

Even better, by asking for and valuing the input of other team members, everyone on your team will know they're important and your culture will become much stronger.

Create Healthy Competition

Funny enough, one of the greatest drivers of a healthy culture is healthy competition. While many companies shy away from highlighting or creating a competitive environment, we find that it keeps people honest, engaged, and excited about pushing forward and doing better. The juxtaposition you often find yourself in is that you have to determine how to build friendly competition while still helping your fellow agents. One of the steps we took, which I borrowed from my old firm, was to install a big whiteboard in the office where we ranked each of the agents based on earnings and production. This has been a really interesting experiment, as the agents don't want you to see them standing in front of the board and studying it. So I often see them walking by, snapping a quick photo of it, and then going about their day.

But I can tell you they know where they stand. And they want to lap the other agents. This healthy competition keeps each agent motivated to do better, sell more, and close deals. However, we balance that out with an open-door policy and an attitude that we're all going to help one another succeed. I see it every single day at Ansley. Agents collaborating and talking about how they can generate and produce. They exchange ideas, discuss what works, and synergistically come together to improve. This healthy internal competition sparks amazing results as all our agents develop their skills and begin producing at high levels.

How to Choose the Right Team Members for the Job

As odd as it might sound, the first step to finding the right team members is to identify what areas you need the most help with in terms of how you think, how you like to work, and your most natural leadership style.

In terms of how you think, are you more of a conventional thinker or natural innovator? For example, what first comes to mind when you think of a networking strategy to build new referrals? Do you think about sending gifts to local centers of influence? Do you think of sponsoring local events? Do you think of hiring a celebrity to host a meet and greet at your office for local business owners and their families? Or do you think of writing a book about your local community and interviewing the "most connected" people in the city to tell you their favorite hidden gem in town?

If your thoughts go immediately to one of the first two questions, you're more on the conventional side. If your thoughts jump right to one of the latter, you're more of an innovator. You need both on your team. That way, you can keep doing what you know works well while pushing the envelope a bit to continuously improve, like we continuously tweak our habits at Ansley. At the same time, you can create space for some of the unconventional and innovative strategies to market your business and consistently improve day-to-day operations.

In terms of how you like to work, would you rather roll up your sleeves and get things done "right" the first time or are you more comfortable delegating work to others, even if it means that some things might not get done exactly how you would have done them? Again, you need both on your team: someone to roll up their sleeves to do the work and someone to make sure all the dots are connected so everything that needs to be done gets delegated to the right person.

Finally, in terms of your most natural leadership style, are you more outgoing and personable or a quiet, lead-by-example type? Understanding your natural leadership style will help guide you in bringing in team members who work best under that type of leadership.

If you're unsure about any of the answers, I highly recommend using the assessment tools we have at BrokeringBillions.com. I use these exact tools to evaluate both my team members and me to make sure everyone I bring in is set up for success from the start. For example, the last thing I want is to bring someone in to handle listings and closings who is a big-picture thinker who can't stand to sit behind a spreadsheet all day.

Even with these tools, finding the right team members can take a lot of trial and error. But the assessments and testing we can do with each team member to identify their core skills can help. They aren't perfect, but they give us a lot of great insights into the roles in which a candidate can thrive. Even if you already have a team in place, these tools can help. You might learn that someone on your team is in the completely wrong position for their natural tendencies and can thrive with a simple shift in responsibilities.

Know Your Audience

This next team-building lesson came from an unexpected source: a listing I almost lost.

It started innocuously enough, with a potential new client, Mo Bunnell, asking me a question I had been asked hundreds of times: "What do you think my house is worth?"

On most occasions, it's the single most important issue anyone selling a home wants to address. Sure, they'll sit there and politely listen to your presentation. But when it's all said and done, the number is the only thing that matters. "How much can you get for me?" Or, more succinctly, "Show me the money."

Right away, I liked him a lot. He seemed intelligent, and I later learned that he had worked to reach the highest level of an actuary, someone who deals with the measurement and management of risk and uncertainty in business. The profession demands a high proficiency in math. His business has now evolved into consulting with professionals on how to develop their business—how to really sell. It was clear he was engaged in our listing appointment. I had only been an agent for a year and was still finding my voice and honing my pitch and craft. But I was gaining confidence and growing my business.

I looked at him stoically, confident I had the right answer. "Mo, I think we should list your home for $600,000." As always, I paused, awaiting the reaction.

He responded, "Well, how do you know that?"

I was ready with my answer, as I always was. "I have sold every house in this neighborhood. I'm the top guy in Atlanta, and I just know your house is worth $600,000! Trust me!" Mo smiled at me, thanked me for my time, and escorted me to the door. I left the appointment thinking I had just signed yet another client. Thinking I was going to put my sign in his yard the next morning.

But something strange happened. Mo called me the next day. "Hey, I'm interviewing a lot of other agents about the house, and I've got some follow-up questions for you. You didn't fully answer my question when I asked you what my house is worth." Confused, I agreed to meet him at his office. Once I arrived, after a bit of small talk, he said he wanted to show me a diagram of the brain. This was a first for me. He took out a piece of paper and drew a big oval on it. He then divided it into four sections. "This is the brain," he said. "For our purposes, it has four unique quadrants." Then Mo showed me that the brain has four main modes of thinking, with two opposing pairs: analytical vs. relational, experimental vs. practical. I'm a visual learner and his presentation really hit my core.

He then said to me, "Look, my tendency is to bias toward experimental and analytical. You crushed the experimental part, brainstorming about all the creative and innovative marketing strategies we could do to increase the exposure and buzz around the house, but man, you majorly failed on the analytical part. I needed data—an analysis of other homes like ours and a +/- reconciliation of how you came up with $600K. All I got from you was a headline and promises. And on top of that, $600K is a round number that sounds made up!" I about fell over, but Mo gave me hope. "Listen, I want to work with you, I just need some data to help me feel comfortable." I understood right away: Mo, as an actuary, lives in the analytical/experimental world. I just needed to provide him with the relevant data to make sure we were both on the same page.

I went back to my office and drew up a detailed comparative marketing analysis for Mo's home. Needless to say, I landed the listing, and since then, I've had an over ten-year personal and professional relationship with Mo. He taught me a valuable lesson in that meeting, one that will stay with me forever. What I learned is to attend listing appointments prepared for pretty much anything. I learned to pick up clues from a prospect from our first contact and adapt to the way they want to buy my services instead of communicating in a way I would buy my services. The prospect puts out these clues from my first interaction with them, and I lean heavily not only on my intuition and gut but also on my emotional intelligence and strong relational skills to form a rapport with the client.

You never know who's going to be sitting across the table from you when you're doing a presentation. Looking back, I realized early on that I'd do really well if I was making a sales pitch to somebody who thought like me, who was more experimental and perhaps more of a dreamer. I was ten for ten with this type of individual. However, it was just a matter of time before I encountered a potential client like Mo who was more analytical, and where I might need to stretch further to connect. And the same is true with your team members and communication. Many times, it's not what we say but how we say it that matters.

Throughout my career, thanks in large part to Mo's help, I've learned when to be logical vs. procedural, when to be empathic and put myself in my client's shoes, and when to just listen.

As I got bigger in my business, I learned that not everybody I'm pitching as a client or leading on my team thinks like I do. They're not all experimental thinkers. They could be more relational or intuitively inclined. I love working with intuitive thinkers. When I show them property, I'm constantly amazed by their ability to visualize what they could do to maximize their house's potential. They love diving into paint colors, landscaping, visualizing how their art could be more effectively placed in the house, and even dreaming about pruning the remarkable boxwood hedges surrounding the back patio.

Now, the truth of the matter is that Mo's house was worth $600K. I wasn't wrong about that. And he listed it for that very price. But what I didn't know then is some of my habits at the time were not serving me. Mo gave me something far more valuable than a commission. He gave me insight into how my programming was failing me, as well as a remarkable tool to understand my thinking style preferences.

I even went through Mo's sales training course and put my team through it as well. My favorite part was getting the detailed results of how I prefer to think, based on a system Mo uses called the Herrmann Brain Dominance Instrument. It turned out I'm pretty balanced in terms of using the four quadrants of the brain, but with a relatively strong bias to experimental, intuitive thinking. I was stunned that I was balanced, but the results ended up making so much sense to me. It explains why I naturally take risks, can zap around from one mode of thinking to another with a bias toward innovation and strategy, and also seem to get along with so many different kinds of people. It explains also how I can skip past some of the details, which is why I've hired people to backfill in those areas. Then, another light bulb moment: we needed to scale these insights across the team. Everybody thinks differently, but few organizations can leverage cognitive diversity as a strategic advantage.

Why? At Ansley, thanks in large part to Mo's guidance, we have deliberately built systems for our in-person meetings, pitch materials, website, and social media—basically any way we communicate—so that we're hitting all four ways of thinking, all the time. We like to think we're coachable. We specifically tailor our *Ansley Collection* magazines to accomplish this—we feature human interest stories, data diagrams, and process steps, in addition to showcasing many of our real estate listings. We also did the same with our office space, designing it to be a very open, airy environment where people's creativity and energy levels can thrive.

I have listed several houses for Mo over the years, and even recently sold him his dream home, a historic house in Atlanta on ten acres, where he has a barn, pastures, and horses. So Mo has clearly had great success in his business life and knows what he is talking about when he teaches about selling. He sets out his system in his book, *The Snowball System: How to Win More Business and Turn Clients into Raving Fans* (PublicAffairs, 2018). In the book, Mo emphasizes the creation of habits that serve your ultimate goal—growing your business and having a great time doing it. "Each time you successfully perform a habit," he says, "you will feel more energized to perform that habit the next time."

One experience, one lesson, and even one interaction can change your habits. For whatever reason, people have this preconception that it takes a village to change habits. That's far from the case. In truth, common sense would dictate change when that change can better serve your immediate and future goals. As an agent, I wanted to land more listing appointments and close those appointments when they occurred. My general practice was to prance right into those meetings and secure a new client because I told them what their house was worth, not because I explained the value to them.

But Mo, who I sometimes affectionately refer to as "The Actuary," shifted my thought process to a much more effective practice. I haven't lost too many listings in my career, but going forward, I wanted to make sure I connected with each of my clients' unique functioning or approach to life. My newfound knowledge gave me a more complete package. In one short meeting, I was able to completely change a habit of mine. All it took was an open mind and one quick lesson.

Building the Team Needed to Achieve Your Vision

Even during my early stages of selling homes, I was aware that no broker can do it alone. I knew I would need the support of others to create a strong infrastructure along the way.

I've built that team to operate at an optimal level and make sure my team members are put in the position to succeed. And when I mean succeed, I don't mean "work harder than the other firms." I mean they're put in a position to help us achieve success *as we define it*. I mean they succeed in helping us achieve my vision for the team.

And that means we aren't tied to our desks seven days a week. I don't work much on the weekends. I'm home usually by 5:00 or

6:00 p.m. We work smarter than we work hard, although we do work hard in the hours we dedicate to our work.

But we do a lot of business. We do a lot of things during the day relative to the company. And we make sure we have the tools and people in place to succeed from a marketing standpoint, from a motivation standpoint, and from an efficiency perspective. We do no "busy" work. We do impactful work.

As I've said before, I'm smart enough to know how dumb I am, so I built a team that fills in my gaps, and I give them the tools and resources to be successful. I'm committed to hiring slow and firing fast. I want people to show me they're the right person to bring into the culture I've built. That can take a while. It requires me to go slower than I want to sometimes. But it has saved me from introducing the wrong people on the team and slowing down our growth, or worse, bringing in someone so toxic when you get to know them that it makes everyone less fulfilled and productive. If someone slips through the cracks and ends up being the wrong fit, I let them go. The way I see it is if they're not the right fit for my team, my team is also not the right fit for them, so delaying the inevitable departure does nobody any good. Cut bait. Find someone else. Let them find a better fit.

Put People First—Whether They're Your Staff, Clients, or Prospects

Julie Harris and I started to innovate together, thinking of creative ways to support our team and build a culture of winning. We touch base often to brainstorm. Julie had the wonderful idea of creating small groups of high producers to meet regularly. We bring six to eight of our agents together and collectively discuss different trends, marketplace activity, and everything in between. Julie leads many of the groups, and we truly believe in the phrase "iron sharpens iron." By bringing these successful agents together and personally challenging them, we not only raise their ceiling we also improve our culture by setting examples for the rest of our team.

This type of collaborative culture, which we strive for at Ansley, stands in stark contrast to most of our competitors, all of whom are basically franchises. Because they have large corporate entities and big money behind them, they often can't be nimble or pivot quickly. With these firms, you're working within a structured template, and the agents can feel like they're handcuffed. This virtually ensures that the work environment will be far more structured and restrictive. Because the firms have big investors to answer to, they can become stiff. We have fewer rules at Ansley on purpose. "Corporate," for us, is almost a four-letter word.

"Our business is about putting people first, which we believe is the greatest driver of success," said Julie Harris, our chief people officer. "To a firm, an agent is their first client—and agents are independent contractors. You are equipping them to go out and sell. You want them to be happy. What most firms don't get right culturally is that they do not connect the dots between marketing, accounting, the agent, the client, the staff, and our business partners—all of the different pieces that have to be connected to make it work. Let's have fun and create a dynamic, supportive, creative environment—everybody does better and lives better. We do that through building a culture that people genuinely want to be a part of. It is a choice, and we make it every single day. No one is here going through the motions. You must leave your crown at the door, work high and low, pitch in and do the work. Everyone is dedicated to being their best, and they demonstrate it each and every day they are at Ansley."

Julie put it best. "Ansley is absolutely about the people—our people, our customers, and everyone with whom we interact on a daily basis," she said. Even though I founded this brokerage firm, I knew from day one that the only chance I had to succeed was to build a team focused on winning together. Julie ensures that our people remain empowered and supported in their endeavors. The trickle-down effect is that our team members are not just happy, but they are heard. They each have a voice that we respect and listen to. It is a two-way street. We aren't just talking at them, but rather opening up the lines of communication to ensure their perspective and wonderful ideas are considered and even implemented.

Set the Mood

Culture is not just what you say, but what people feel. It's an attack (in a good way) on your senses. You should smell, hear, see, and feel culture. At Ansley, we did our best to pick the perfect office space for our flagship in the middle of an exciting part of Atlanta. Cool stores, great restaurants, and fun places to grab a coffee or a drink after work surround our office. If you were to walk into our space, you would immediately see floor-to-ceiling windows with lots of light coming in. We're always piping upbeat music throughout the office, and we empower our team with industry-leading technology and all the resources they need to succeed. Each office we've opened has a similar vibe and feel to be "Ansley."

At Ansley, we encourage team events, outings, and interaction. You can feel it in the air. Our office has a great deal of open space, and even the single offices feel wide open, with multiple agents sharing space to support collaboration and interaction. Think about your office space. Is it welcoming? Open? Or does it consist of physical barriers? Does it push for interaction or seclude employees away from one another? Your senses are the first thing to connect to an environment. Think about walking into a restaurant and smelling great food. Or stepping on a beach to see a beautiful sunset. You will feel an immediate sense of pleasure. We want that same connection in the workplace.

Tell Your Story

One of the most important things a real estate agent can do is tell a narrative. Think about what it might be like to sell a house. Every house has a story, right? A potential buyer walks in and wants to know the details. They want to know who built the house, when it was constructed, and maybe even any historical facts that give it life. As opposed to just saying, "Hey, this is a five-bedroom, three thousand-square-foot house," it's "Hey, this is a happy house, you know? It was built by this builder with these materials. And the neighborhood is great for kids. The backyard is really great because, you know, this family plays kickball every day . . ." If you're able to connect the house with a story, it's easier to stand out, particularly if someone is looking at a bunch of houses. So at Ansley, we teach our agents to be storytellers.

Stories are how we as realtors and human beings connect. Oftentimes, great cultures start with tremendous stories. Your team members should always know your company's origin. They should know where you came from and how you got to where you are. Without it, you're just brick and mortar. You're just infrastructure. The story is where the heartbeat is. It's the DNA and the very fabric of your being.

Author Sue Monk Kidd said, "Stories have to be told or they die, and when they die, we can't remember who we are or why we're here." Sounds pretty dramatic, right? Well, that's because stories matter a great deal. If you can't tell your team where you came from, they likely won't understand where they're going. But if they hear the story and actually connect with it, then they will do all they can to ensure the next chapter is as good as the ones that came before.

So it prompts the question: how do you tell your story? That's an important question for any leader to answer. We tell ours through our culture. Through how we interact with one another. Through how we serve our clients. Every one of our team members knows that I started Ansley to get away from the antiquated brokerage houses that have ruled over the market for at least the past thirty years. They now see it in our office, our staff, our resources, and our success. The story lives because we live. The story continues because we work hard to ensure it does. That's how you tell your story and keep it alive.

Utilize "Small Groups"

I learned this concept early in my real estate career and have found it to be a valuable tool for our team members. Small groups are when we assemble a few agents, maybe six to eight, into a collaborative group. They each have one agent at the helm, and the group consists of similar producers. They meet regularly and exchange ideas and guidance.

These small groups help to accomplish two important goals:

1. They build bonds between agents.
2. They have their own culture, goals, and rules.

By creating their own set of rules, goals, and targets, these small groups are empowered to do things their own way. It ends up being a company within a company. Each small group has its own culture and identifiers. No two small groups are the same, just like no two agents are the same. We eventually learned that many of these agents travel with their small groups, regularly spend time together outside of work, and become extraordinarily close. I've seen some of the greatest production at Ansley come from the collaborations and mini think tanks that occur in these small groups.

Spread Love and Acceptance

Funny enough and sad at times, far too many companies do not demonstrate to their team members that they're accepting and understanding of diversity and different personalities. At Ansley, we made it a pillar of our organization. We value people from all backgrounds, experiences, and origins because they offer us insight and the opportunity to learn from one another and grow. I couldn't imagine building a brokerage firm of people just like me. I'm unique, and having people like our chief motivation officer and Julie, my chief people officer, by my side (who are very different from me) acts as a remarkable complement to my style of leadership.

As of the publishing of this book, we recently ran a campaign entitled "Love is Love." Working with a local nonprofit that supports diversity in the workplace, we celebrated the differences among us all and stressed the great value of welcoming diversity as a game changer for us all. It's important, especially in today's workplace environment, that we not only talk about inclusion but really practice it. Your work environment should be a healthy place where you can truly enjoy yourself and grow. You shouldn't have to hide something like your beliefs, sexuality, religion, or anything else for that matter. Our culture should, if nothing else, scream of acceptance and allow people to just be people. As you spread love and acceptance, you'll find that every team member will feel empowered to do great things.

Celebrate Success

As obvious as it might seem, few companies take the time to celebrate success. If you're going to create a strong culture, then you have to ensure you're pointing out and then actually rewarding great accomplishments. If you expect your team members to truly leave it all on the field, then you must not only show them you recognize their efforts but also do your best to reward those same efforts. At Ansley, we created the Circle of Excellence, which consists of recognizing our top-selling agents every single year. We take these high performers on an all-expenses-paid trip to a scenic location outside of Atlanta. We spend time together, learn from one another, listen to great invited speakers, and just celebrate their success over the past year. It's important that we show our hardest workers that they matter and we appreciate all of their dedication to our team.

But we aren't just celebrating success at the end of the year. We do it throughout the year. Julie has crafted several different awards that often coincide with a small gift. We dish them out on what seems like a monthly basis when team members demonstrate strong leadership, innovative thinking, customer service, love for team members, and pretty much any other meaningful component that makes up our culture. We love celebrating these small but impactful accomplishments, and we've heard our team members feel appreciated and recognized when we do. Far too often organizations live in the problem. They're quick to point out when someone does something wrong or drops the ball. But on the flipside, they're painfully slow in pointing out when a team member knocks it out of the park or goes above and beyond. If you want to build a strong culture, then you should do so by not just saying "thank you" but actually showing how you appreciate the effort.

There are so many different ways to build a strong culture. I've outlined just a few of the many above. Culture should be personal in the sense that you should create something that's absolutely representative of your core and fundamental principles. It should feel right. It has to be natural. It cannot be forced. Like a connection between two people on a date, culture has to just feel like it has been there forever. Sure, there are steps you can take to ensure you create contagious culture. But it has to be reflective of who you are and what you want your company to be. In some ways, I would call it your identity. To that end, carefully plot out your culture like you would your own image, because in the end, it's a reflection of just that.

Keep It Simple

Are you a believer yet? I hope so. I am a big proponent of building a thoughtful and strategic culture. Andrew Mason, founder of Groupon said, "Hire great people and give them freedom to be awesome." That pretty much sums it up for me. It's really a two-step process:

1. Hire great people.
2. Empower them to be awesome.

Those are the two steps that lead to strong culture. One without the other and you have no chance. They aren't complementary; they're totally reliant on one another. An empowered environment filled with unhappy or negative people will never gain momentum. And a great set of people without a nurtured environment will remain stagnant as well. But magic can happen when the two intersect with one another. It is a remarkable occurrence. I've been fortunate enough to witness it firsthand here at Ansley. And now that I've gotten a taste of it, I realize more than ever that I have to do all I can to protect it. You will likely feel the same way once you start to see how a contagious culture can impact your organization. The best part about it is that a little can go a long way.

I bet you have heard of the biological concept of regeneration. In science, this is a process of renewal, restoration, and growth. This concept is remarkably relevant when it comes to culture, as it's evidence of this in motion. The more culture you introduce into your organization, the easier it is for these habits and this attitude to renew, restore, and grow. Culture breeds culture. We started Ansley with the idea of imparting a strong sense of culture within it, but what we've seen occur is that the small seeds we planted on day one have been watered by each of our tremendous team members. We offered them the opportunity to develop our culture, and they are all now great examples of it. I rest easy knowing that our staff believes in our narrative, loves our culture, and wants to talk about it to anyone who might listen to them.

Chapter 6:

Rounding Out Your Cast

I n 2009, when I was just getting going in the Atlanta market, I had a bunch of competition, and the real estate market was in shambles. But I needed to get the word out so I could get more listings.

How was I going to jump on the scene? At the time, it was just me. I didn't have a team. I didn't have a budget. I was building everything grassroots. But I knew I wanted to be the top broker, so I committed to playing the part from the start. In other words, I'd do what the best brokers did from the start, giving 100 percent of my energy and attention to becoming the top agent in Atlanta.

I knew that I'd need to know everyone in Atlanta if I wanted to be the top broker. There were way too many big real estate brands around who had been in the market for decades. I couldn't just put up a billboard or send out the typical flyers to make people think of me first. I needed to know people and build an army of relationships with people all over Atlanta who would act as my brand ambassadors when anyone mentioned buying or selling a house.

So that's how I looked at Atlanta. Everyone in the city was already on my team, even if they didn't know it yet. In my mind, if you could influence a real estate transaction in Atlanta or help me become a better agent, you were already on my team. You just didn't know it. I put everyone on my team. Everyone. Tommy the barber. The valet guys at Chops. The valet guy at Blue Ridge. Financial advisers. Accountants. Everyone.

They became part of my sphere. We would play golf together. I'd take them to dinner. I'd take them to lunch. I became a genuine friend with everyone in town and did everything I could to help them become successful. And they did the same for me.

If you want to Broker Billions, you need everyone in your area to know who you are—and think good things about you. In this chapter, I'm going to show you how to identify the people you need in your cast and how to get them talking about you.

Be Methodical

When I tell agents to get into the mindset that "everyone" is already on their team to help them sell real estate, some of them push back. Some have read marketing books or taken business classes that suggest aiming at "everyone" is a bad thing. They say something to the effect of "if you sell to everyone, you sell to no one."

I get it. What I teach seems to run against conventional wisdom. But the problem with conventional wisdom is it tends to build conventional businesses. I don't want you to be a "conventional" agent. I want you to be a top agent. And that means getting everyone in your area thinking of you first when someone's looking to buy or sell a house. I want you to get every listing. I want you to "double-dip" on every possible transaction. I want you to be featured in the next edition of this book, just like Thad Wong, Mark Spain, Johnny Ussery, Keene Reese, Glennda Davis, Holly Parker, Jonathan Spears, Julie Faupel, Rob Thomson, Leigh Marcus, Josh Anderson, and Elizabeth DeWoody.

So, yes, I want everyone talking about you. But I don't want you talking to everyone. Quite the opposite. Instead, I want you to be methodical, to build deep relationships with two groups of people who collectively touch everyone in your area: super influencers and secret influencers.

You don't need to know everyone, but if you know all of the best super influencers and secret influencers, you'll directly or indirectly have everyone in your area on your cast, thinking of you first every time they want to buy or sell a house.

Building Relationships with Super Influencers

Of course, everyone wants to get on the radar of the super influencers. You know who they are: (1) people who know everyone in town and usually have a fancy title—like restaurant owners or country club managers, and (2) people directly involved in real estate transactions—like mortgage brokers and developers.

Building relationships with super influencers is great. But everyone wants to get to know them. For example, a single developer can get you dozens of listings a year. And even if their listings aren't perfect, if you're showing dozens of listings, you're going to meet a lot of people who are looking to buy homes. You might end up selling them another one of your listings or even get the listing for their existing home if they haven't hired an agent yet. Similarly, mortgage brokers can connect you directly with clients but also introduce you to other super influencers they work with.

To build relationships with these super influencers, you need to be creative and bold. A useful resource for identifying gifts that get noticed by people who can buy whatever they want is the book *Giftology: The Art and Science of Using Gifts to Cut Through the Noise, Increase Referrals, and Strengthen Retention* by John Ruhlin. In it, Ruhlin talks about giving people gifts they'll display and talk about. For example, Ruhlin likes to send people custom Cutco knives. Unlike many people, Ruhlin doesn't suggest customizing it with your logo so the person will remember your name every time they use them. In fact, wealthy people will likely not even use the knife if it has someone else's logo on it. They'll likely regift it. Instead, Ruhlin suggests engraving the knife with the recipients' names on them. When you do, they'll be much more likely to use the knife regularly, including when company's over. And when company compliments the knife, they'll often say, "You'll never guess who gave this to me. My real estate agent." As of this writing, you can get a custom-engraved signature Cutco knife with a gift box for $170. And the beauty of sending Cutco knives is you can send additional knives over time to build them a set.

Going Big—And Green

As he shares in his most recent book, *Save Your Asks*, in 2014, my partner in *Brokering Billions*, Chris Tuff, was obsessed with Facebook. He had worked directly with Mark Zuckerberg and his team before most marketers knew what to make of it, but it had been a while since he had met Mark Zuckerberg, and he wanted to reconnect.

Having not spoken with Zuckerberg in years, he felt his connection slipping. Zuckerberg was well on his way to becoming one of the richest people in the world, so reaching out with an email or phone call likely wouldn't get his attention.

He needed something more. Then one day, he watched an interview with Zuckerberg about Facebook celebrating its tenth anniversary. During the interview, Zuckerberg mentioned that he was in the market for a new grill. The second Chris heard those words, he sprang into action. He happened to have a connection to the grill company Big Green Egg's head of marketing. So he called up his connection and asked if he could send Zuckerberg a Big Green Egg.

Through his relationships at Facebook, he was able to connect with Zuckerberg's assistant and sent a Big Green Egg with a card that read, "Here's to an amazing 10 years at Facebook. Thumbs up from your friends at 22squared." (Chris's advertising agency.)

After some drama about how Zuckerberg would get the Big Green Egg home, Chris heard through the grapevine that he loved and used it. About four months later, when Zuckerberg used Facebook Live for the first time, right behind him sat the Big Green Egg.

Chris's connection at the Big Green Egg made such a big gesture easier than it would have been for others, but that's not the point. The point is that Chris paid attention to something Zuckerberg was interested in (a grill) and took action. You can do the same in your world too. It might not be a Big Green Egg or Cutco knives but listen for opportunities to go big with a gift that people use, display, and talk about. You'll stay top of mind. And the next time another agent sends them some cheap marketing gift, they'll immediately think about you and how you went above and beyond.

As Chris says, "Take action. You might not know what it will lead to when you do, but I can promise you that doing nothing won't lead to anything."

Be Memorable with Memorabilia

Another example of "displayable" gifts includes sports memorabilia they'll hang on their walls. For example, years ago, a friend sent an autographed picture of Michael Jordan hitting the final shot to win the NCAA championship for the University of North Carolina (UNC) to a lawyer who's a partner in a large firm in New York City (who also graduated from UNC). He paid $500 for the photo at the time. The lawyer was floored and immediately displayed it right behind his desk. Years (and several office moves) later, the photo still appears in the background of every picture taken in his office, and my friend is the subject of conversation every time someone asks him about the Jordan autograph.

Look for opportunities to be meaningful in your gifting too. For example, another friend of mine once attended a personal growth conference. During the conference, the host talked about the impact that the book *Think and Grow Rich* by Napoleon Hill had on him as a teenager.

"When the book first came out in 1937, they only printed five thousand copies, perhaps not expecting the book to be very successful. Almost immediately, the publisher had to print more and more copies and the book has sold millions of copies since then," he explained.

He continued, "I think about that first run of five thousand books all the time. One of these days, I imagine being in an antique bookstore and running across one of those copies. The interesting thing is that the original text is now in the public domain so anyone can download a PDF of the original version. But there's something about that original run of five thousand books that is so special."

My friend, who is a master of building deep relationships with influential people, filed that information in the back of his mind and began searching for one of those five thousand books when he got home from the conference. He found a few that were in poor condition or missing dust jackets or promotional materials that were inserted in the book at the time and a couple that were in pretty decent shape. One was listed on an antique book dealer's website for $3,000. It was in great condition and had both the dust jacket and the promotional materials included. There was no doubt in his mind that the conference host would cherish this version. So he reached out to the book dealer, confirmed the book's authenticity, and negotiated the price to $2,500. Seven years later, my friend can trace at least 25 percent of his business back to the relationship he built with this guy. To this day, the guy proudly displays his first print, first run *Think and Grow Rich* right over his shoulder on every Zoom call he's on and uses it every time he tells the story about how that book changed his life, including how my friend found and bought him the first print, first run copy after hearing the story for the first time.

While $500 or $2,500 might seem like a big price to pay for a gift to someone with whom you're just hoping to build a relationship, it's a much better use of your money than peppering people with stress balls, polo shirts, or mugs that have *your* branding on them, knowing they'll either give them to their kids or throw them away. And $170 for a knife that they will use, display, and talk about on nearly a daily basis is *dirt cheap*. A no-brainer.

Build Bridges

Like many successful brokers, Jonathan Spears encourages you to look at your relationship building as building bridges in your community, even with other agents. So many average agents think of other agents or brokers as competitors. And, although I want all the listings and would love to find buyers for my listings through internal marketing, I know everyone wins in the long term when I help clients sell their home fast and for the highest price. And that means finding the *right* buyer, even if that's someone who isn't on my list.

The way Jonathan describes his approach is that he sees himself as a connector, a matchmaker of sorts. "Part of being a connector is connecting yourself to people who are smarter than you," he says. "We connect buyers to great properties. We connect sellers with the right buyers. To do that well, we need to embrace consumer-facing sites like Zillow, other agents in the area, and even the community as a whole."

Jonathan doesn't see those sites and people as competition. He sees them as additional resources he can use to serve clients well. "We should be collaborators. But that requires you to build great relationships with your clients and others in the community. Play the long game. Respect other agents. Make an emotional connection with them. The more you do, the bigger your team of referral partners, collaborators, and buyers will be. And that's a great way to sell more homes and add even more value to your clients."

Getting All the Most Impactful "Secret Influencers" on Your Cast

Although super influencers carry a lot of weight in their areas, there's another group of people who impact just as many people— if not more—that way too many agents ignore: secret influencers.

Secret influencers are the people who might not carry the same business or political influence as the local business owners, lawyers, and CPAs. And they might not directly impact as many real estate transactions as local developers. But they regularly interact with your ideal clients by nature of their work. These people are the bartenders, valet parkers, servers, car detailers, hair stylists, barbers, and others who interact with your clients regularly.

When you treat secret influencers well, they can become some of the most powerful marketing cast members at a fraction of the cost of traditional marketing.

So how do you find and build relationships with secret influencers in your area? It only takes four simple steps.

First, ask yourself where the clients you want go regularly Where do they eat? Where do they get their hair done? Who details their cars? Where do they get their daily coffee?

Second, arrange your schedule to frequent the same places. Eat lunch where they eat lunch. Eat dinner where they eat dinner. Get your hair cut where they get their hair cut. Get your car detailed where they get their car detailed. Get coffee where they get their coffee. Make sure you show up looking the part too. If you want to be seen as *the* luxury real estate agent in the area, show up looking like someone who could be trusted to sell a million-dollar home. If you show up looking like a slob, nobody will see you as a successful, high-end agent.

Third, treat the staff at these places well—and tip them *big*. Because there are so many secret influencers in your area, you're not going to be giving them all custom knives or high-end sports memorabilia. But take great care of them by tipping them big—and I'm not talking 20 percent either. I'm talking much higher than that. If you buy a $4 coffee, give them $10 and tell them to keep the change. If your lunch bill is $25, give them $40 and tell them to keep the change.

Fourth, let them know you're the best agent in town and take care of anyone who refers people to you who end up buying or selling a home. Give them a stack of business cards, too, so they can hand them to anyone who mentions buying or selling a home.

In my case, I wanted to land the best listings in town, so my wife Jen and I would eat dinner at the fanciest places in town. When we got there, we made sure we didn't sit at a corner table, away from everyone. We'd sit right in the middle of the bar, make friends with the bartenders, treat the staff with the respect they deserved for all their hard work, and, of course, tip them big time.

Guess what happened? The bartenders ended up being on our cast. Every one of them knew we were selling real estate. They knew we were committed to becoming the best agents in town and would work our butts off to make sure our clients got into their dream homes.

Before long, the bartenders started introducing us to people looking to buy or sell homes. They'd introduce us to the person in the corner of the bar who they learned was in town to look for a home. We would do that *every single night*.

When you do this every single night, it doesn't take long to build relationships. The first night, they didn't know us, but we struck up a cordial conversation, asked them about themselves, and tipped them well. The second time, they remembered us. The third, they remembered our names. By the fifth or sixth night, they knew a lot about us, and we knew a lot about them. We became friends and looked out for them by bringing people with us to the bar or telling people to go to the restaurant and ask for them.

In exchange, I told them I'd take care of them if they'd give my business card or brochure to anyone they overhear mentioning anything about moving to or from the area or buying or selling a house.

I did the same with the valet guys. I treated them great. They were awesome guys working hard and looking to make money. So I'd give them $100 or $200 tips every time I saw them along with a stack of my magazines and told them to stick one on the passenger seat of every luxury car they parked. And they did.

Let Your Desk Get Dusty

If you're hanging out at the right places and building relationships with super influencers and secret influencers, it's only a matter of time before you start to control the market. But you need to get out from behind your desk. You need to leave your office. Let your team handle all the transactional work. Let their desks stay nice and clean from all the paper sliding across all day.

But your desk should get dusty. You have no business eating lunch at your desk. I don't care how busy you are. If your desk doesn't get dusty, you're spending too much time in the office and likely doing tasks that you have no business doing if you want to Broker Billions. You might be working hard but you're not working very smart. The smartest you can work is to go build relationships with super influencers and secret influencers.

The 3 Cs of Connection

Another important lesson Chris Tuff shares in *Saves Your Asks* that I use to Broker Billions is what he calls, the "3 Cs of Connection."

If you can master the 3 Cs, you can create relationships with just about anyone. As Chris explains, "The fastest way to create relationships is through the power of 3 Cs: currency, curiosity, and confidence."

Your currency is all the things you know, own, or control that other people want. It could be access to a country club or high-end wine. It could be knowing how to become more influential in their community. What do you have that other people want? Look for opportunities to talk about these things in conversations with people you want to build relationships with.

Use curiosity to learn about the person you're trying to connect with. Ask questions about them and listen for things you have in common and opportunities to use your currencies to help them achieve something they want.

Finally, exhibit confidence when connecting with potential cast members (really, everyone). This is more of a learned skill than anything else and might take some repetition. Practice this with every interaction.

If you consistently work on the 3 Cs of Connection, you'll build a strong reputation as someone others want to connect with—and make connections for.

Sustain, Don't Just Create Relationships

"Creating relationships is easy. Sustaining them is difficult."
—Chris Tuff

Finally, as you round out your cast, don't forget to sustain all the relationships you've developed. If not, all the goodwill and top-of-mind awareness will dwindle fast. In other words, the success you achieve because of your cast will be determined by a combination of the number of people on your team who know, like, and trust you and how frequently you touch base with them to stay fresh in their minds.

That's important to know because creating relationships is fairly easy, but sustaining them is more difficult. But how do you sustain all these relationships and still make it home in time for dinner (or to take your family or significant other to dinner to continue to round out your cast)?

In this case, it's all about two things: (1) making regular touch-points, and (2) becoming a super connector for your clients, another concept Chris talks about in great detail in *Save Your Asks*.

When it comes to regular touchpoints, make sure everyone gets on your email or mailing list. Just let them know you're going to send them some information from time to time. They won't mind.

When you sell a home, make note of how long your clients plan to stay in the home. Do they have kids entering high school? Maybe they'll want to downsize when the kids move out. Do they not have kids yet? Maybe they'll need a bigger home or a house with a yard in a few years. Stay in touch with them and use anniversaries as an excuse to send them a nice gift. I like to send past clients gifts on their home purchase anniversaries such as the first, fifth, and tenth anniversaries of a house closing. I'll also send all clients quarterly gifts, like a Frisbee and suntan lotion when summer comes around. And when winter comes around, we send them chocolates and a note to enjoy them on cold winter nights.

With respect to becoming a super connector for your clients, one of the easiest ways to add value to clients is to be *the* go-to person they reach out to when they need anyone or anything. And between all the connections you make as you round out your cast and the clients you meet in your business, you'll soon become the most connected person in your area. Then, all you need to do is make *mutually beneficial* introductions.

The best part about becoming a super connector by making mutually beneficial introductions is that it only takes a minute to get top of mind with the people you introduce. A past client asks you whether you know a good CPA. You reach out to a talented CPA who has been a good source of business for you and ask whether it's okay to make an introduction. They say yes and you make an email connection. You got multiple touchpoints with the past client and CPA and added value to them without you having to do any work.

And if you sell 50, 100, or 200+ homes a year, like I do, you should get to know what a lot of people in your community do for work. Over time, between your clients and your cast, there's almost nothing you won't be able to help with. Then they'll think of you every time they need something—including when they or someone they know needs to buy or sell a home.

All these people will become your brand ambassadors if you maintain your relationships and stay top of mind. That's how I've been able to double my business and then double it again. And again. And again. And that's how you can do it too.

Chapter 7:

Billion-Dollar Reputation

"I've learned that people will forget what you said, people will forget what you did, but people will never forget how you made them feel."

—Maya Angelou

As I sat down to begin pulling together the content and stories to write this chapter, my phone rang. I didn't recognize the number, which in my world is often a good thing because it's often a potential new client or referral partner whom I haven't yet met—a "money call," as I describe them.

Like many ADHD people might do, I picked up the phone, excited about the possibility that this could be another money call and comfortable with the idea that answering the call might delay my writing for a bit.

"Bonneau Ansley?"

I didn't recognize the voice on the other end of the line—a woman with the poshest British accent I've ever heard.

"Bonneau, we've never met before, but you come very highly recommended by people I trust."

At that moment, I knew this was, in fact, another money call. She was in the process of downsizing and needed to sell her home and buy a condo. And I was the broker for the job, but not because of my flyers or sponsorships around town or any other type of marketing. I was the broker for the job because of my reputation.

Your reputation is the glue that connects all the pieces of your business, from your vision to your marketing, and everything in between. It's what makes people confident in hiring you. It's what makes people refer you to their friends, family, or clients. It's what makes or breaks you over the long term because no matter how big a game you talk, nobody will refer someone important to them your way if you have a reputation that doesn't match your words.

If you build a Billion-Dollar Reputation, you'll be well on your way to Brokering Billions.

You Already *Have* a Reputation; Is it the One You Want?

I once heard someone say that the definition of a reputation is simply what other people say and think about you when you're not around. In other words, you either already have a reputation as an agent or broker or nobody is talking about you.

Your reputation starts building before you sell your first home. Even if you're just getting started, you have a reputation based on what you've done in the past. If you already have a reputation in real estate, that means people around town are talking about you in connection with selling homes. Of course, this can all be good or bad. It's possible that your reputation isn't exactly what you want it to be.

But if nobody is talking about you outside of your immediate network, that means you might as well not exist, at least when it comes to selling homes. Again, this can be good or bad, as well. If I had to choose between having a bad reputation or no reputation when it comes to selling homes, I'd probably choose to have no reputation because you're starting with a blank canvas, can control it from the start, and can build a positive reputation pretty quickly.

If you have a reputation for being sloppy or unprofessional, you have an extra obstacle to overcome as you build your reputation into what you want it to be.

Either way, the good news is you can easily create the reputation you want. You just need to draw a line in the sand, decide what you want people to say and think about you when you're not around, and then act like that person from this day forward.

Want them to think of you as *the* best luxury agent? You need to *be* the best luxury agent and make sure everybody can tell you're committed to being the best and most successful agent. As petty as it might sound, people really *do* judge a book by its cover. You need to portray yourself as professional, successful, and committed to helping people buy and sell luxury homes.

What does that look like? Well, if you show up driving an old broken-down rust box with fast food wrappers all over the seats, what does that suggest about your success to people? No luxury homeowner is going to want that car parked in front of their house during an open house or pulling up with people for a showing. Upgrade your car to something that lets luxury home buyers know you're either already successful or committed to being the top luxury agent in your area. You don't need a brand new Bentley but drive a car that demonstrates luxury and professionalism and keep it clean so people see you as organized.

When interacting with people, go above and beyond. Show up on time for meetings. Look well-groomed and dressed professionally. Ask potential buyers and sellers a lot of questions. Get to know them personally and professionally. It astonishes me how many agents show up, talk about themselves, and tell them the same things every other agent will tell them about how they'll sell their property. None of that makes you stand out.

You need to be more intentional about showing up, being different, and going all in to build the reputation you want, not the one you developed by accident. Do it with clients. Do it every time another agent brings a buyer to you. Do it with every super influencer and secret influencer you come across. Decide how you want people to talk about you and then be that person.

If you haven't yet sold your first home, think about how you want people to talk about you to their friends, family, and colleagues. Then give them that experience so they will talk about you that way. Then do it again with your second home. And your third. And fourth. And so on. When you do, your business will multiply and your reputation will build the way you want it to.

Not Your Typical "Open House"

In 2011, I was still finding my way around selling homes in Atlanta. Yes, I was the top-selling agent in town, but I hadn't even cracked the surface of what I wanted to build. I wanted to be known as *the* luxury agent around. I had built my reputation pretty quickly as a go-to agent but was still looking for a showstopper that would cement me as an innovative and outside-the-box agent who could move luxury homes in any market.

Late that year, after the Atlanta Braves informed one of their players that they had traded him, I'd get a call that changed the trajectory of my business forever. Unfortunately for the player, he was having a hard time selling his Atlanta home: a beautiful five thousand-square-foot estate with five bedrooms, six bathrooms, a pool, a patio, a cabana area, a finished basement with a wine cellar, a cigar room, and more. The property was beautiful, but it was empty and was proving hard to move.

After unsuccessfully listing the property with another agent, he found my name. I had been selling real estate in Atlanta for a couple of years at the time and had been positioning myself as the best agent in Atlanta to move luxury homes. I had also become known as a creative, hardworking, and trustworthy agent who priced homes correctly and had a knack for finding buyers. I told him that an empty five thousand-square-foot home is not easy to move, so we'd need to get creative but that I was the best in the business and could make it happen. He told me he trusted me and gave me the listing.

There I was, just a couple of years into selling homes in Atlanta, and I had this big $3 million five thousand-square-foot house with nothing in it to sell. It was one of my first big listings. I thought to myself that this was my best opportunity to showcase my creativity and blow it out of the water. So I decided to be different. I wouldn't just call a staging company, fill up the house, and schedule open houses. That's what average brokers did. I wasn't average. I was the best.

What do the *best* do when it comes to selling homes? They don't just fill them with furniture and artwork. They fill them with people too—and not just *any* people; they fill them with potential buyers. So I reached out to the owner of a local art gallery and said, "Man, I've got a great opportunity for you. Why don't we do a venture party to help you sell some artwork? I've got this beautiful house with nothing on the walls. You bring in some beautiful artwork and invite all your top people who have spent over $10,000 on art to an event they won't soon forget. I'm going to bring in all the Atlanta elite and will pay for the entire party." They were in. I then reached out to a Maserati dealership and told them about the event. They agreed to sponsor some of the event and bring some nice cars out front for test driving. Finally, I contacted the local news and told them about the house and event. This guy was a big deal in town and the news was happy to come out to report.

Altogether, the event cost me around $15,000. I had great food and drink, along with *millions* (and I mean *millions*) of dollars of art on the walls. Obviously, this *wasn't* your typical "open house." People all over the city wanted to be at the event, even if they had no interest in buying a house. And, coincidentally, that's exactly who bought it—someone who came to look at the art and had no interest in real estate. I found them in the living room and sold them the house.

Be Bold and Become the Talk of the Town

You might not have an empty five thousand-square-foot house to move. And you might not have a local art gallery and Maserati dealer to partner with. But if you want to build the reputation of a billion-dollar broker, you *need* to be different. You can't just do what the typical broker does when selling homes. You need to do things worth talking about. To this day, I have a story to tell about how I moved an empty five thousand-square-foot house fast and even got featured on the news for doing so. While that was just one of my first big listings, it was a story that earned me a reputation as *the* agent to move luxury real estate in Atlanta.

When I tell newer agents about that story, they often ask, "What's the entry-level version of that story? Like, for those of us who are newer, if we land a luxury listing that needs a little extra attention, how can we create a mini version of your baseball player house party?"

Here's the deal: If you want to Broker Billions, you need to go all in. You need to go for it. Want to be the luxury agent in your area? Don't look for the "entry-level" version of anything. Go big. You might not throw a $15,000 party at a $250,000 house in a market where houses move in a weekend with bidding wars. But you might do that in a softer market with a $2 million house for a client who wants you to help them upgrade to a bigger house when that one sells.

You need to make sales happen. You need to bring buyers to your listings. You need to be proactive. You need to go big when you have an opportunity to up level your reputation. I don't care if you're doing a little bit of volume now. If you act like someone who does a little volume, you're going to get stuck doing a little volume. You didn't create all that margin and time freedom in your day building your team and rounding out your cast to sit back and do nothing. You need to go all in and act like the agent you want to be.

To be clear, I don't mean to lie to people. I mean to act like the top broker in the area. Do what top brokers do. If you want to Broker Billions, you've got to be all in or thousands and thousands of other agents will go all in.

You've got to put everything on the line when you've got somebody interested in listing with you or buying a property you're selling. You can't let that person out of your sight. Woo them. Send them some flowers. According to Rob Thomson, "You need to send something *immediately*, within hours of the meeting." I make sure to send them an orchid or something like that right away—no later than the next day. I've probably bought more orchids than anybody in Atlanta because everybody I meet gets an orchid for me. And when they're interviewing other agents after me, that orchid is sitting right there in the kitchen.

How to Maintain a Billion-Dollar Reputation

> *"It takes 20 years to build a reputation and five minutes to ruin it. If you think about that, you'll do things differently."*
> —Warren Buffett

When interviewing the top brokers from all around the country, I asked each of them to name the one characteristic you need to compete at our level—to be *truly* successful in real estate.

In the words of Rob Thomson, the one characteristic you need is "a combination of honesty and drive." In other words, you can't "fake it until you make it" when it comes to being the best agent in the area. You need to *be* the best broker in your area and then do everything you can to make sure everyone knows about it.

"You really have to be authentic to who you are," adds Holly Parker. "As I say in my book, you got to fly your freak flag. Find out what is unique to you, what makes you, you, and, whether it's a mess or not, make your mess your message. Figure out what makes you unique. Mine is that I've always been kind of an open book, so to speak, and I'm okay with sharing my weaknesses, and I'm okay about talking about struggles. When Facebook came out so many years ago, all these images of perfect moments drove me crazy because they're not real. And I just thought, *This is not good for people. If you're going to show these perfect moments, I want to see the moment that is not perfect.* Just be real. Why are we trying to be these things that we're not? That's me. I'm a truth bearer of, 'it's not all good.'"

The beauty of what Holly has done is that she's mastered the art of showing the good, bad, and messy without coming across as disorganized or unprofessional. That's an important point because this is *not* about being fake. It's *not* about being someone you're not. It's about being your true, authentic self but being intentional about how you authentically present yourself to the market. Being real and having problems doesn't make you unprofessional. It makes you more relatable. You just need to let people know that you are the top agent, despite your challenges. In my case, I'm open about my dyslexia and ADHD, yet nobody is worried that I won't be the right person to help them sell their luxury home. And Holly's openness about her true, authentic self doesn't impact her negatively either. If anything, it's a positive.

If you ask any top agent about the importance of authenticity, honesty, and drive, they'll all tell you the same thing. If you want to make a single sale, you might get away with a little white lie. If you want to become the top agent in your area, don't even think about being dishonest.

To Broker Billions, you need to move a lot of property. Remember, it took Julie Faupel 60 homes to hit $327 million in sales in 2021 in the white-hot, high-end Jackson Hole, Wyoming, market. And Rob Thomson hit $445 million in 2021 with a little less than 100 transactions. And, of course, it took me 497 transactions to sell more than $900 million in 2021 and 2022. You don't get to that volume without playing the long game.

When building your reputation, you need to decide who you want to be and then stick to it for good or for bad. Decide what values are important to you. Decide what culture you want to promote in your team. Then commit to it, even if it costs in the short term because you should never look at yourself or your career in the context of making one sale at any cost.

This takes a lot of self-discipline, but you can undo years of goodwill in minutes if you aren't careful. So if you spend a bunch of money to promote a house only to have the sellers decide they're not going to sell it anymore, don't flip out or pressure them into selling. That news will spread fast. Instead, genuinely wish them well and let them know you're ready to help them when the time is right. They'll come back around. You've got to play the long game on everything you do. Missing out on one or two deals is not worth hurting your reputation.

Treat Your Reputation with the Same Intensity as Everything Else

"How you do anything is how you do everything."

—Jesse Itzler

I think many people max out at 85 percent effort from what they do. It's the "good enough" mentality, and it drives me crazy.

You've got to break through that and get to 100 percent effort. Give your reputation everything you've got. That goes with everything you do. You create this reputation that people talk about, from your effort to your professionalism to the creativity with which you sell property. That'll get people talking about you and all the amazing things you did to help them. That ends up multiplying over time.

When I first got going, I focused on gaining experience and providing top service with the goal of becoming the go-to luxury home broker. I knew that people's experiences with me would spread around town. And they did, quickly building the reputation of providing the best service and busting out even more with a reputation as an innovator with what I did with the baseball player's house. I didn't have to wait until the event for my reputation to spread, though, which is how I was able to be the number one agent in Atlanta my first year. Reputations can build quickly, even back then before social media and online reviews were so popular. Nowadays, reputations can build even faster.

I didn't have all million-dollar listings when I first got started either. I had a mixture of lower-priced homes with some higher-end ones mixed in. It didn't matter if the house was $200,000 or $2 million, I wanted people to remember me as giving them the best experience and service, so I treated them all the same.

Fortunately, it wasn't hard for me to give high-end service to people no matter how much their house was worth or how big their buying budget was. As many people with ADHD know, empathy is one of the hallmarks of living with ADHD. And I knew that buying and selling a home was likely the biggest and most important transaction of my clients' lives. So it was pretty easy to put myself in their shoes and treat them and the transaction with the importance they deserved.

That's true in any industry. If you buy a car and have a great experience, you'll likely go back to that dealership in three or four years when you're ready to trade it in. If you had a terrible experience, you'll go somewhere else.

Continue that experience and service after the transaction too. In the car industry, the top salespeople call their customers regularly to tell them about new models, new deals, or anything else that's relevant to the customer.

The same is true with selling houses. The constant touch keeps people talking about you to their friends and family and coming back to you next time they want to buy or sell a home.

Keep Track of Everything

When it comes to Brokering Billions, information is one of your most valuable assets. This applies to every piece of the puzzle, from how you price homes to how you present a home to a potential buyer and everything in between. For example, if you know your buyers are looking to expand their family, what do you look for in a home to show them? Do you look for a small home on a busy street with no yard? Of course not. You look for homes with more space, a nice backyard, and maybe even on a cul-de-sac. Agents do this naturally. It's second nature. They don't want to waste anybody's time sifting through houses that won't match the family's needs.

The same is true with building your reputation. The more information you have at your fingertips, the better you will be at building and maintaining a strong reputation. You don't need to be high tech or a master researcher to be able to collect and store information in a way that's readily available to you. If you look behind my desk at the Atlanta headquarters of Ansley | Christie's International Real Estate, you'll see a series of black and red books with dates on the spine, starting from 2004 and continuing to the present.

I keep track of everything in those books. I mean, with dyslexia and ADHD, I have to, or I'd forget. They're my journals of every conversation I've had going back even before I started selling real estate in Atlanta. In those books are every thought I've had about selling real estate, every transaction I've completed, and every meeting I've had. You name it, if it could help me build deeper relationships with people and sell more real estate, it's in one of those books.

Combined with my calendar where I schedule every appointment and my emails, which track my communications in real time, those books give me a tremendous advantage over other agents. If I'm about to meet with someone, a quick search on my calendar and emails shows me when we last spoke. Then, I can flip to that day in my journal and see exactly what we talked about. It's low tech, but it works well for me, as the act of writing with a pen helps me cement the information in my brain for quick recall. You don't need to use a pen like I do. You could use a running Google Doc to take notes. But use *something* to take notes during or immediately after every meeting so you never lose any information.

In addition to being a great way to never lose any information, it's also a great way to be able to look back in time to spot trends and be reminded of conversations you had with people. I'm constantly looking through my journals going back a couple of years or so and calling people I met with whom I haven't spoken with in a while. I'll just call and see what's up with them.

As strange as it might sound, that extra effort can turn into a lot of volume and gives me a big database of information to pull from.

Always Be Branding

Branding is everything and everything is branding.

In the 1992 film *Glengarry Glen Ross*, Alec Baldwin played Blake, a sales consultant brought in to help a sales team increase their effectiveness. Although I wouldn't suggest taking his tone with your team, his introductory speech to the sales team he was brought in to support has gone down as one of the most popular scenes in film history, making "A.B.C. A-always, B-be, C-closing. Always be closing. ALWAYS BE CLOSING!" one of the most popular quotes alongside it.

In our world, we can't think of branding as something we do. We need to think of it as part of everything we do. When we invest time, money, and effort into building a billion-dollar reputation, every piece of doing business with us needs to be consistent with the reputation we want to build. Everything we say and do makes a statement about who we are in the minds of the people around town.

If, like me, you want to be known as the luxury agent, you can't skimp on business cards, your website, mailings, marketing materials, social media profiles and content, or gifts. You need to make your brand match your reputation everywhere.

Don't skimp on paper quality for your flyers to save a few bucks. Don't send a cheap gift to a new or existing luxury client. Send something straight out of the *Giftology* book—something they will wear or display in their home. Otherwise, you'll look cheap, and the attention you'll get from sending those flyers or gifts will be both short-lived and the opposite of the attention you want to receive.

Remember, starting today, you *are* the agent you want to be. You just haven't made the sales yet.

So, ask yourself, what would a $100 million agent do? What would a $100 million agent's flyers, gifts, business cards, websites, cars, clothes, shoes, and hair look like? How would they look when they step out of their car? Yes, that means spending some money. But it's an investment. Don't spend it frivolously but invest in upgrading your reputation because you can quickly make all that money back and then some when you double, triple, or even 10x your volume. But you won't be able to double, triple, or even 10x your volume if you keep doing what you're doing. You have to think and act differently if you want to achieve different results.

Ask yourself what a $100 million agent's team would look like. Would the agent be a lone wolf doing everything from making copies to meeting clients? Of course not. Doing everything yourself is terrible branding for someone who wants to build a reputation as a $100 million agent. Clients expect you to have a team.

And what about that team? Would a $100 million agent tolerate unprofessional or unqualified team members? Of course not. They would make sure clients receive the same level of professionalism and care from everyone they get in touch with on your team as they do from you. Agents with that level of success make sure they hire the right team members, train them well, give them the tools they need to do their job well, and make sure they present themselves well to clients.

How about rounding out your cast? Would a $100 million agent stay in the office all day pushing papers, eat a ham sandwich at their desk through lunch, and work until midnight? They would not. Their desks get dusty because they spend their days around town, meeting clients, local influencers, and super influencers.

So what does that all mean? It means you need to think, act, hire, and spend like a $100 million agent starting today. Yes, that might be scary. But what's even scarier to me is spending the rest of your life tiptoeing the line of burnout, working way too hard for way too little money. What's even scarier than that is tiptoeing that burnout line for years or even decades longer than you want to because you can't afford to retire. And what's even scarier than that is working so hard you spend all your healthiest years and your kids' formative years in the office.

The sooner you start thinking and acting like a $100 million agent, the sooner other people will think of you as a $100 million agent. That's critical to your ability to get the listings you want. People won't give you their listings if they don't truly believe you're the right person for the job. And no amount of "I promise I can do it" can overcome a bad reputation.

Be the agent you want to be starting today. Own it. Go big. And be consistent.

As a friend of mine always says, "Consistency is the best productivity hack. You might get lucky once or twice but, over the long term, your results come from what you do consistently."

Every morning, wake up and tell yourself, "Today, tomorrow, and every day moving forward, I am a $100 million agent." Then act like a $100 million agent all day long. Keeping that top of mind throughout the day will help maintain your focus on all the mindset and practical steps in this book that will help you achieve your goals.

Give Back

If you want to be seen as an important member of the community, you can't expect your relationship to be a one-way street. The community will give you millions of dollars in commissions over time if you build the right reputation. But if you're only collecting commissions and not giving back, you'll quickly be seen as a taker or slimy salesperson.

I recognize that not all people are natural givers. Some people worry that giving—or giving too much—will jeopardize their own security. In my experience, the opposite is true. I'm fortunate to be a natural giver. I get more joy from giving away $100,000 to a worthy cause I believe in than receiving $100,000 more in commission, so incorporating giving into my business from the start was a no-brainer. But I know when you're first starting out you might worry that you don't have enough margin to give.

In my experience, even beyond the good you do in the world, giving is one of the best investments you can make for your business and personal life. Over time, what you give comes back to you many times over. It's not linear. You won't always know that someone's hiring you because you sponsored a team or built a local sports field. But it comes back and builds a deep two-way relationship with your community that pays off big time.

If you're just getting started, choose a cause or two in your local community to support. In my case, it's important to me to give back to local causes that mean a lot to me. I love Atlanta. I love the people of Atlanta. I want to be known as someone who cares as much about his community as he cares about anything. So, in addition to giving back to causes regularly, I give a portion of my commission from every sale to an organization looking to give back to Atlanta and the people of Atlanta. I do that both from the personal side and as a company. From the day I started Ansley Real Estate, I made a company pledge to Children's Healthcare of Atlanta that for every sale we do, we'd give something back to the hospital. And we've given them a lot of money since we started.

We let people know how we incorporate giving into our process too. We tell our clients and prospects that we won't just sell their house for more money and in less time, but also that working with us helps improve the lives of many families through our pledge to Children's Healthcare of Atlanta. People love that there's a greater purpose involved when we sell their house.

By giving, not only do you get to help people and build a deeper meaning and importance to every transaction you complete you also build your reputation as someone who gives back to the community.

Protect Your Reputation through Your Culture

Finally, it's equally as important for you to make sure your internal reputation matches your external reputation. If you want to be a $100 million agent who's known for being an important member of the community, you can't be fake. You can't be one person to the outside world and another to your team. You will quickly crash and burn.

Protect your reputation by being the same person internally as you are externally. Structure your internal culture to reflect how you want the world to see you. And make sure your team projects that same reputation both internally and externally.

In other words, everyone on your team should project the same reputation to each other, to you, and to the community.

This starts by building a culture for your team that reflects the reputation you want to build. And it continues by making reputation just as important in the process of how you evaluate yourself, your business, and your team members as any other key performance indicator.

When we interview an agent to work at my company, they need to buy into what we're doing and know how we do what we do, how we give back to the community, and how we make sure we sell a lot of real estate but what we're doing is not about the sale.

If people don't truly buy in, they won't make it past the interview process. If they somehow make it through, they'll end up leaving quickly because everyone in the company protects our reputation.

Chapter 8:

Using Billion-Dollar Marketing to Get Noticed, Stay Ahead of the Competition, and Generate Listings on Autopilot

There's a saying in marketing that the best place to hide a dead body is page two of Google search results. Think about it. How many times do you click to see what's on page two? If you're like most people, almost never. In other words, if you're on the second page of Google search results, you might as well not exist.

This phenomenon says a lot about our society. People generally choose one of the first solutions they come across, even if it's an imperfect solution. Thus, the goal with any marketing activity needs to be for you to become the first person someone thinks of when the idea of buying or selling a home comes up.

In an ideal world, you'll be the first name in search results, the first person who comes to mind with people around town, and the first person who shows up when people look on social media.

Here, we'll build upon all that work to spread the word about what you do everywhere potential clients check when looking for an agent.

Before we do, consider these stats from the National Association of REALTORS® 2021 Profile of Home Buyers and Sellers:[8]

- Sixty-eight percent of sellers found their agent through a referral from a friend, neighbor, or relative or used an agent they had worked with before to buy or sell a home.
- Eighty-two percent of recent sellers contacted only one agent before finding the right agent they worked with to sell their home.
- Fifty-three percent of sellers used the same agent to purchase a home, as sell their home, a share which rises to 85 percent for sellers who purchased a new home within ten miles.
- The typical seller has recommended their agent twice since selling their home.
- Twenty-seven percent of sellers recommended their agent four or more times since selling their home.

Although the profile includes a lot more data, I wanted to highlight these five points for a few reasons.

First, as important as it is to build your reputation online and on social media, more than two-thirds of people still found their

---

8   National Association of REALTORS®, "Highlights from the Profile of Home Buyers and Sellers," www.nar.realtor, 2022, https://www.nar.realtor/research-and-statistics/research-reports/highlights-from-the-profile-of-home-buyers-and-sellers.

agent through a personal referral, and more than 80 percent contacted only one agent before moving forward. That means all the work you've done to build a strong culture, get intentional about your reputation, and build relationships with people around town gives you a head start when it comes to marketing. That, alone, will help you generate listings.

Second, more than 50 percent of sellers used the same agent to buy a home (and 85 percent if they purchased within ten miles of the home they sold). That means, more than one out of every two clients you get from any source will hire you for more than one transaction at a time.

Third, the typical seller recommends their agent to two other people after selling their home and more than 25 percent have recommended them to four or more people. That means all the work you're doing to keep in touch and stay top of mind with clients can pay off big time. If you combine this third point with the second one (that more than half and up to 85 percent of sellers will use you to also buy their next home), it means that each of these referrals will generate between 1.5 and 1.85 transactions.

And all of this will already be taking place when you apply the other strategies in this book. You'll stand out in your town. You'll build and maintain a strong reputation. And you'll stay top of mind with people around town and the clients who are primed to send more clients your way.

Before You Spend a Penny on Marketing

Before you start hiring a marketing firm or ordering thousands of high-end flyers, make sure you put marketing in the right place.

As with reputation, always remember that marketing is everything and everything is marketing. In other words, the work you do in the first seven chapters *is* marketing. If more than 50 percent of clients will hire you for their second transaction, how you serve them *is* marketing for the second deal. If the average client refers you to two people and more than 25 percent will refer four or more people your way, how you serve clients *is* marketing. *Everything* you do is marketing.

Frankly, you can make a lot of money and sell a lot of homes using just the first seven chapters of this book. You can be one of the best agents in your area with just that in place plus a modest social media presence that matches your reputation.

Most agents won't do half of what you've already started doing when working through the first seven chapters. In fact, many of them skip over the first seven chapters and go right to marketing. Think about that for a minute. Imagine what would happen if you started spending money marketing yourself as an agent without knowing what you want to build and putting yourself into a position to serve clients well by having support and focusing on your greatest strengths. Maybe you think for a few minutes and decide to position yourself as the go-to luxury agent. You create marketing campaigns that showcase you as the high-end, service-oriented agent in town. You tell people you can sell their houses faster and at a higher price. You say you can help get deals to actually close. People love your marketing, and leads start coming in.

Then what? Can you follow through on that promise? Most agents couldn't, at least not without having started doing the work in the first seven chapters of the book. Again, you don't need to already have a big team. You don't need to already have the best network in place. You can build that over time. But you need to be able to deliver on the promises you make in your marketing, or your reputation will get real bad real fast. As a friend of mine says when it comes to marketing a business, "Why would you want more people to know about your business if the service stinks?"

That's why you can't forget to do the work in the first seven chapters if you want to Broker Billions. You can't just skip over setting your vision and building a strong team and culture that can follow through on the promises you make with your marketing. That work ensures the leads you get from your marketing turn into clients and those clients hire you for their second deal and send those two to four-plus referrals your way.

So, remember, every time you leave your home, you're marketing your business. Every time you talk with your team, you're marketing your business. Every time you go out to eat, you're marketing your business. Every time you drive around town, you're marketing your business.

Everything is marketing and marketing is everything.

But if you want to Broker Billions, you need to do more than just letting your day-to-day activities get the word out. You need to combine that with world-class, innovative marketing,

Billion-Dollar Marketing

Billion-Dollar Marketing doesn't need to be complex. It doesn't need to be expensive, either, at least in the context of the potential return on our investment by finding a single buyer and landing one additional listing. Because we can make a lot of money from the sale of even a single additional house, even high-end marketing is really dirt cheap.

So what does Billion-Dollar Marketing look like?

First, it's consistent. You need to be consistent with everything you do. The life of the typical social media post is seconds. Yes, it stays on your profile forever. But it hits people's feeds for a matter of seconds. Even viral social media posts die down in a matter of hours or days. What about more traditional marketing, like a flyer or listing book? Well, if done right, you might get your book on someone's coffee table for a while or your flyer pinned to their corkboard or taped to their fridge. But, especially with flyers, unless your materials stand out, you get a glance and then they move on with their life.

Second, it's everywhere. That means multiple places online and multiple places offline. Be where your clients and referral sources are. Get your branding wherever you can. Online, don't just stick with one source. Make sure your website is the best around. Make sure it gives you data you can use, like Rob Thomson gets from his website when people register. And then make sure you use that data consistently, like when he got Tony Robbins on the phone within minutes of his registering on Rob's website. On social media, be on all the relevant sites.

Third, it's multimedia. From video to Frisbees, flyers to custom pickleball hats, shirts to social media posts, and everything in between, be everywhere your clients are, online and offline. With so many distractions in people's lives these days, we can't expect them to be drawn to us with one touchpoint. We need them to think of us multiple times so we stay top of mind.

Finally, it's targeted. Yes, we need to be consistent, everywhere, and multimedia. But the purpose of what we do is to build our reputation, reinforce the image we want to project, and move houses. That means, before we approve any marketing efforts, we make sure they are consistent with our reputation, reinforce the image we want to project, and will help us either attract more buyers or sellers.

If we want to be known as a positive contributor to the community, we might choose to send gifts from local stores. And if we want to move more homes, we make sure our posts showcase properties, promote referral partners who are part of our cast to stay top of mind, and showcase homes for sale in a creative way that lets people experience the best parts of the home.

The Everywhere Economy

There's no better example of being *everywhere* and expanding and adjusting as attention shifts than Glennda Baker who works with me at Ansley | Christie's International Real Estate.

When reality TV broke into the real estate world, *everything* about selling homes changed. Many old-school agents who have been in business for one hundred years don't like reality TV because it puts a whole different light on real estate.

Two years ago, Glennda had just a few followers on social media. Today: more than one million. She's in a whole different league because she's like a reality TV star. People want to work with her because she can expose their houses to millions of people on TikTok, Instagram, and all the other popular social media channels.

Glennda takes advantage of the thirst for reality TV-type content and the changing landscape of where people consume content. She produces high-quality videos where she talks directly with her followers, sharing behind the scenes about what's going on in her life and the real estate industry.

For example, in one video she shared a short story about how she sold a $3 million home because of a bottle of water—yes, a bottle of water. Curious how she could have achieved that? That's exactly why she's so successful online: everybody wants to know the story. Then, when they see the video, they click follow and watch everything she does.

If you really want to know how she turned a bottle of water into a $3 million listing, I'll share the short story. Before I do, what I love most about the water bottle story is that it demonstrates how important it is to be consistent, everywhere, multimedia, and a strong member of the community. (It also demonstrates that effective marketing doesn't need to be complicated . . .)

It all started six years before she turned the water bottle into a $3 million listing. Glennda had connected with a local school that was holding a teacher appreciation event and looking for sponsors. Glennda happily sponsored the event by providing bottles of water with her face and information on the labels, an investment that cost her forty-seven cents per bottle.

Six years later, one of the attendees hired her to list her $3 million home. When Glennda asked how her new client got her name, the lady said that she saved the bottle of water to remember for when she sold their home.

In Glennda's words, "I have gotten more business from those bottles of water . . . I bet you I've made $1 million from those bottles of water."

Let's park here for a minute and evaluate what happened here. Glennda bought a bunch of water bottles with her face and contact information on them. She regularly gives them away because, obviously, everyone drinks water. And, while the story she shared is about one $3 million listing, she estimates that she's made $1 million just from giving out bottles of water. Not only that, but she turned her water bottle story into social media content that builds her following and deepens relationships with her audience across multiple platforms. She posts videos every single day. They're simple, minimally produced, but heavy on interesting content.

To summarize:

- she consistently gives out low-tech but useful "marketing materials" with her contact info on them (water bottles),
- they cost next to nothing (forty-seven cents each), and
- she sponsored a local event.

The result? In just a few years, she has built a *massive* audience and her social media posts reach millions of people.

Being everywhere doesn't need to take more time than if you concentrate on one or two areas. And it shouldn't take more of *your* time. In fact, you could record one fifteen-minute video and turn it into dozens of pieces of content by doing the following:

- Putting the video on YouTube
- Having someone write blog posts for you based on the videos
- Stripping the audio and turning the video into an audio podcast
- Creating short quote images based on the videos to share as images online
- Cutting short clips that you can edit into video posts for various social media sites
- And that's just the beginning

With the right team in place, you can easily be everywhere without *you* having to be everywhere. That's where everything's going. I call it the "everywhere economy." If we want to get anywhere, we have to be everywhere. But we don't need to do everything ourselves. You can outsource, delegate, and automate almost every piece of the puzzle so you can do what you do best and what moves the needle the most for your time.

Although the "everywhere economy" existed pre-2020, during the COVID-19 pandemic and beyond, it accelerated, as more people took to social media to communicate with each other and their attention shifted even more away from traditional media.

As a result, the traditional way to market your houses and business has changed dramatically. And that's why it's so important to build a team that can handle most of the work selling homes while you round out your cast and build your brand and reputation.

Being Social without Being Fake (or Tied to Social Media All Day)

If you think building an audience like Glennda's takes hours a day or requires you to be perfectly coiffed and put together, think again.

Glennda is regimented. She films all her TikTok and Instagram videos one day a month for eleven hours right from the comfort of her own home. At first, she was able to record about a dozen videos. The next time she got twenty. The time after that was twenty-one. Today she can record sixty videos in a single day.

"I shoot at my home because I feel comfortable," Glennda explains. "I want to be able to change my star outfits so I don't have fifty videos all in the same star sweater. This is my space. I feel comfortable. If I want coffee, I can get it. If I want a bottle of water, it's right there. Whatever I want is at my fingertips."

Her monthly filming session starts at 7:00 a.m. when the videographer and lighting guy arrive and start setting up. At 8:00, Glennda participates in a ten-minute "call to greatness" with her business coach. After, she frames out the morning recording session using a Google Sheet that she uses to keep track of ideas she gets for videos throughout the month. On her phone, she has a shortcut to a Google Form she can fill out when inspiration strikes. That form populates a single Google Sheet so all of her ideas remain organized in one place.

After they plan the morning, they record from 8:30 until 11:30 straight. At 11:30 they break for an hour for lunch. After lunch, they plan the afternoon videos for thirty minutes and then shoot again from 1:00 to 7:00 or 7:30.

Yes, it's a long day. But it's one day a month, and she can get up to sixty videos recorded in that one session. I asked Glennda what she would recommend to agents looking to build their own social media platform:

> If you are an agent looking to start on video, don't be worried about how I do it. Figure out how you can be efficient and effective with your time. If I shot a few videos every day, that would take two to four hours out of my real estate day. I don't have that luxury. I make money selling houses. So I record once a month and then post my videos every morning, typically between 6:30 and 9:30 in the morning. I have a system and a process for everything, and I feel like that's been the key to my success.

That said, what I implore the real estate agent community to do is to understand that you have never, ever before in your life had the opportunity to create the narrative, to control the narrative of your community like you do today.

Social media gives you an opportunity to be "local news" about real estate in your community. On national real estate news you'll hear it's a recession or a real estate downturn. While that might be true, what's going on across the country has nothing to do with what's going on in your neighborhood. You can be the real estate news for your community with video and social media. So, I implore you, with every fiber of my body, if you take nothing away from me, I want you to take away the phrase "I can control the narrative for the real estate market in my community by video today."

Video gives you an exponential reach that you never had before going to the country clubs, sending out mailers, going to the PTA meetings. You could never reach the amount of people in your community that you can reach today with video.

Don't wait to be perfect either. Just start experimenting, see what sticks and make sure it's authentic to yourself. I have built such a large following by being myself. In fact, being imperfect is probably the number one thing people like about me. I've got this crazy hair. I'm fifty-five years old. I've made plenty of mistakes. I'm not trying to hide any of that. And that's a big part of what makes people attracted to me on social media.

Glennda's advice leaves you with two big takeaways. First, once again, systems, processes, and routines win the day. Glennda's routine might work well for you, or it might not. But the secret to being successful with social media without having it take you away from selling is to create a system and process that works for you. Second, social media allows you to control the narrative about real estate in your community. Don't let the national media control the market. Get on social media and use video to let people know what's really happening in your area.

Google Yourself (but Do It Right)

If you haven't Googled yourself, there's no telling how much money you've lost. Why? Because what's the first thing people do when the bartender you build a relationship with gives your card to them? What do you think that person is going to do before calling you?

They're going to google you. They'll check Instagram, Facebook, YouTube, TikTok, and other places. But the first thing they'll do is google you. When they do, what will they see?

Will they see a sloppy, unprofessional, or even nonexistent online profile? I hope not. Will they see a professional and consistent online presence that demonstrates the level of professionalism, skill, and dedication you want them to think about you? I hope so. If not, it's not too late.

But before you go googling yourself and get the wrong impression, you need to know one thing: your Google results might look different from their Google results when they search for you. Why? Because Google often customizes search results based on your online activity. So, if you google yourself, do so in a private browser window to get a sense of what people will see about you.

For example, before this book comes out, searching "Bonneau Ansley" in a private browser window shows the following results on the first page:

- BonneauAnsley.com
- AnsleyRE.com
- My LinkedIn profile
- My Instagram profile
- My Facebook Page (with my five-star rating showing)
- Four videos featuring me on YouTube
- An article about me on ElegantIslandLiving.net
- Several images of me from various websites
- An article about me on ModernLuxuryInteriors.com
- My ChristiesRealEstate.com profile

Shortly after this book comes out, the Amazon listing for this book and my Amazon author profile might bump a couple of those sites off the first page, so it might be different when you search than when I search.

But my point is that my search results reflect my reputation and show people that I'm dedicated to serving clients well. And if you click on any of those search results, you'll see the same thing too. My Instagram will be professional and updated. The same with my Facebook and LinkedIn profiles.

If you want to Broker Billions, you need to walk in the shoes of prospective sellers, buyers, and cast members. What will they do before hiring you or referring someone to you? Among other things, they'll google you. Make sure when they do, what they see is consistent with what you say.

Demonstrate Your Unique Value to Become the Only—and Obvious—Choice

One challenge facing agents and brokers these days is the perception by many people that all agents are the same or that agents don't earn their commission. This is a big problem for agents who aren't willing to go the extra mile to demonstrate their value.

Of course, some people just aren't going to be convinced, even with stats provided by the National Association of REALTORS® that show that homes for sale by owner typically sell for far less than the selling price of other homes.[9] But most people, when presented with facts about how agents can sell homes faster and for more money, at least listen.

And, if we can show them we are likely to sell their house even faster and for an even higher price than the average broker or agent, we will become the only choice for them. Remember, 82 percent of recent sellers contacted only one agent before finding the right agent they worked with to sell their home. That means they're unlikely to shop around much once they have reason to trust us.

To overcome this challenge, everyone you get in touch with needs to know what makes hiring you the right decision. For example, with me, I let people know how I start marketing a house before it even hits the market and can often sell it before we list it because of my "coming soon" campaigns and internal marketing to my list of buyers and sellers. I also let them know how I pre-

---

9   National Association of REALTORS®, "Highlights from the Profile of Home Buyers and Sellers," www.nar.realtor, 2022, https://www.nar.realtor/research-and-statistics/research-reports/highlights-from-the-profile-of-home-buyers-and-sellers. ("FSBOs [for-sale-by-owner homes] typically sell for less than the selling price of other homes; FSBO homes sold at a median of $260,000 last year, significantly lower than the median of agent-assisted homes at $318,000.")

pare a house to be listed, including how I take all the stress away by bringing in my team of professionals to complete all the items we need to do to maximize the home's value and make sure it sells fast. This includes staging, pre-listing inspections, pine straw, fresh flowers, gutter and window cleaning, getting current on any pest treatments, and ensuring the pool is in good repair.

Within two minutes of meeting me, potential sellers, team members, and cast members know exactly why working with me is a good idea for them. I'm not a commodity. I'm someone who sells your home fast and for top dollar. I can often even find you a buyer with a single email and a handful of phone calls. By the end of the first conversation with people, I'm the only and obvious choice for them to hire.

Control the Inventory

If there's one thing more valuable than having a big list of buyers, it's controlling the listings. If you control the inventory in the market, you've got a major advantage over everybody else. Not only can you show buyers a lot of inventory easily but you can also do a lot of double deals, where you represent both the buyer and the seller and don't have to split your commission with everyone. I've done a lot of double deals.

It's really hard for an agent who doesn't have any listings, who is a buyer's agent. Every week they're competing with ten other buyer's agents on one house. That is not a fun way to work.

So what does that mean for you? Focus the bulk of your marketing on potential sellers. Yes, buyers are important. You can collect buyers in many ways, such as by requiring people to register on your site to view properties, like Rob Thomson does on his site.

Building a list of buyers is valuable. But if you only represent the buyers, you will always be at the whim of the people who control the listings.

If you control the listings, everyone will be at your whim. And when you do effective pre-listing marketing, you can even complete an entire double deal transaction without the house *ever* hitting the market.

When You Get a New Listing

When I talk about Billion-Dollar Marketing, I'm really talking about marketing two things: yourself and your listings.

So far, I've concentrated on marketing yourself. That's where most of your efforts will be spent, to spread the word about working with you. That's important.

But I also want to briefly mention marketing your listings, because the better you get at marketing your listings, the better you'll get at marketing yourself. In other words, how well you market houses makes it easier to market yourself. Thus, I want to make sure you prepare, premarket, and market homes better than anyone in your area.

First, make sure you create a list of "must dos" for preparing a property for sale, such as staging, landscaping, and cleaning gutters, and have trusted partners to complete each of those who will get their part done fast. If you want my list, visit BrokeringBillions. com and you can download it for free.

Second, start building a buyer's list right now if you haven't done that. Make people register on your site when looking at listings. Create downloadable materials or information buyers want and add it to your website in exchange for people's contact info.

Use that list to promote your listings to potential buyers before the house officially hits the market.

Third, conduct a "coming soon" marketing campaign if you don't have a ready buyer for the house already. Let local agents tour the home ahead of it going to the market.

Systematize everything you can do to prepare and market a new listing before it goes live. Create a standard operating procedure document that spells out exactly what you do, how you do it, and why it's important. That document can serve as powerful marketing content when talking with potential sellers about why they should hire you. And the stories you collect from selling homes for top dollar before they hit the market will help you convert even more potential sellers into clients.

The Best Listings Go to the Best Marketers

I spent the first seven chapters of this book helping you develop the mindset, business model, and reputation of a $100 million agent. Now I'm telling you that the best listings go to the best marketers. So was all that work a waste? Of course not. Remember, everything is marketing and marketing is everything.

You need to incorporate marketing into everything you do until it becomes a natural extension of who you are. For example, just last week, I pulled up to a red light. My kids were sitting in the back seat. Next to me was a beautiful gold Lamborghini. Of course, my kids knew exactly what was coming. I was going to get that guy's attention and make sure he had my contact info.

They've seen me do this hundreds, if not thousands, of times in different situations, and it never gets less embarrassing for them, apparently. Sure enough, I motion to the guy to roll down his window. He does. And I tell him, "Man, that's a nice car! I sell houses. You need a house to match that car!" and then gave him my number.

If you're going to be in this business, you need to be out there doing everything short of tattooing "I sell real estate" on your forehead. You need to tell everyone what you do and be methodical about how you get the word out, how you structure your team, and the unique value you provide to your clients.

Otherwise, the agent with the best marketing will get the listings. They might completely screw up the relationship. They might completely fail. And you might end up getting the listing seven months later after the contract expires, especially in a tight market. But in a strong or neutral market, it's likely the agent with better marketing will sell the house, albeit slower and for a lower price than you would have, and the client will be lost forever.

So, if you don't want to waste all that time and effort you put in working on your mindset, casting a vision, developing goals and habits, building a team, rounding out your cast, and building your reputation, you can't stop now.

It's not easy to hear those words sometimes, but I'm not here to make you feel good. I'm here to make you *money*. And, to make money, you *have to* outmarket the other agents too.

Conclusion and Next Steps

Eight steps. That's all it takes to Broker Billions.

Is that oversimplified? Perhaps. But the truth is it's not complicated. You just need to be different.

You need to build your business differently than other brokers do. You need to commit to aiming big and casting a vision that might intimidate you at the beginning.

You need to decide what life you want to live. You need to decide what kind of agent you're going to be.

Then, you need to *be* that agent starting today.

If you want to be a $100 million agent, you need to act like one right now.

Yes, that's scary, but you'll never be a $100 million agent if you make decisions like a $1 million agent.

What does that look like?

You need to commit to working smarter, not harder. You need to surround yourself with people, systems, and software to take over all the tasks you shouldn't be doing. Then, you need to make sure you give those people all the tools and support they need to do *their* best work. That will give you a house-selling machine that delivers a consistent experience at every point in the process, from prospecting to post-closing.

With that in place, you round out your cast, build and protect your reputation, and flex your marketing muscles. Everything you do is designed to build relationships so that you're no more than one degree of separation from every homeowner or home buyer in your community.

You give back to your community and make mutually beneficial connections between clients and other locals to stay top of mind and help your community thrive.

You build a professional presence online and use software to capture leads and build a strong internal list of buyers so you can continue to improve your ability to find the right buyer for every home that lists with you.

And you're consistent. Your social media profiles are professional and constantly updated. You regularly send out thoughtful gifts to past and present clients and others.

You know that everything is marketing and marketing is everything.

You want to control *all* the listings.

And you know that the best listings go to the best marketers.

Does that sound like a lot? The truth is that it's not. I had to figure all of this out on my own and I still made it home for dinner with my family and crushed every sales goal I set.

And I'm not smarter or better than you. I'm just smart enough to know how dumb I am and did two things.

First, I got mentors. I had guidance from the likes of Rob Thomson and learned everything I could from him and others who had businesses like the one I wanted to build.

Second, I focused all my time on actions that came naturally to me, a dyslexic, ADHD misfit who was supposedly destined for mediocrity. I discovered my areas of strength and eliminated, delegated, and automated anything that didn't fit right in my wheelhouse.

If I can figure out how to do it, there's no reason you can't do it, too.

And with this book and the additional tools, resources, and mentorship opportunities I made available to you at Brokering-Billions.com, you can instantly be light-years ahead of where I was when I first got started and didn't even really know what questions to ask my mentors.

You can instantly have a system and even mentorship opportunities available to you to connect even more with me and other agents looking to Broker Billions while still making it home in time for dinner.

As you go, be sure to share your progress with me. Just visit BrokeringBillions.com and send me your story. Who knows? Maybe I'll be able to feature *you* in the next edition of *Brokering Billions* to inspire the next generation of agents to take action and build a better life.

About the Author

onneau Ansley is an Atlanta-based entrepreneur and one of the top-selling real estate agents in the US. He has built, developed, and sold property throughout Georgia and South Carolina over a twenty-year career. In December 2015, Bonneau launched his eponymous brokerage, now called Ansley | Christie's International Real Estate, to offer his clients, team, and Atlanta a locally owned, more personal, relationship-focused real estate experience supported by leading-edge technology.

Bonneau's real estate and business accolades include

- Over $900M in personal production in 2021 and 2022
- Number one agent in Georgia, team category, *Wall Street Journal*

- Youngest agent in Georgia to reach $1 billion in career sales
- Named 2018 Entrepreneur of the Year by the Buckhead Business Association
- Recipient, *Wall Street Journal* Real Trends Top Team in the United States
- Who's Who in Luxury Real Estate "Outstanding Rookie" award 2013

Bonneau and Ansley | Christie's International Real Estate are honored to support Children's Healthcare of Atlanta with proceeds of home sales being donated to their local hospitals. This giving is a process that helps our communities and gives Bonneau an opportunity to contribute significantly to a community partner with aligned values.

As a fifth-generation Atlantan, Bonneau's resources are invaluable and provide a matchless network of colleagues, friends, developers, equity partners, clients, and more.

Bonneau and his wife Jen live in Buckhead with their two children, Blakely and Beau, and two dogs. Members of Passion City Church, the family is very involved in the community and loves traveling together, especially to Sea Island, Georgia. Bonneau is a proud member of YPO Southern 7, is a board member of the Georgia State Golf Association Foundation, and is an active alumnus with his high school alma mater, Woodberry Forest School in Virginia.

A free ebook edition is available with the purchase of this book.

To claim your free ebook edition:

1. Visit MorganJamesBOGO.com
2. Sign your name CLEARLY in the space
3. Complete the form and submit a photo of the entire copyright page
4. You or your friend can download the ebook to your preferred device

Print & Digital Together Forever.

Snap a photo

Free ebook

Read anywhere